SERVANT OF LOVE

E. LE JOLY

SERVANT OF LOVE

*Mother Teresa
and her Missionaries of Charity*

1817

Published in San Francisco by

HARPER & ROW, PUBLISHERS

New York   Hagerstown   San Francisco   London

Imprimi Potest N. D'Souza, SJ
          Calcutta Provincial, the Society of Jesus
          12th February 1977
Imprimatur Lawrence Cardinal Picachy, SJ
          Archbishop of Calcutta
          15th February 1977

FIRST UNITED STATES EDITION
LIBRARY OF CONGRESS CATALOG NUMBER: 77-15874
INTERNATIONAL STANDARD BOOK NUMBERS: 0-06-065215-2
                              0-06-065216-0 pbk.
SERVANT OF LOVE was first published in England under the title WE DO IT FOR JESUS

78   79   80   81   82   10   9   8   7   6   5   4   3   2   1

Contents

Foreword

This book is not a complete biography of Mother Teresa – she does not want one to be written; neither is it a full history of the Missionaries of Charity, the religious congregation God inspired her to found – which can only be written at a later stage, when all the relevant documents are made available.

This book tries to depict the beginnings, aim and spirit of the Missionaries of Charity, as seen by one who was connected during many years with Mother Teresa's foundation.

'Servant of Love' owes its inspiration to Mother herself; it is the only book she has asked to be written to explain her objectives to her numerous friends and helpers all over the world.

This narrative is based on Mother Teresa's own words, in public or in private conversation, her letters, the Constitutions she framed for her Congregation, and the testimonies of eye witnesses who worked with her, especially during the heroic first years.

I wish to express my gratitude to Father Céleste Van Exem, Father Julien Henry, Mr Michael Gomes, Monsignor H. Eric Barber, Brother Andrew, and several of the Senior Sisters, who may not like to be singled out by name from among their Sisters. I owe much to the spoken testimonies of these witnesses, who all took an active part in the establishment of the Missionaries of Charity.

I also wish to thank Mrs Ann Blaikie, Miss Jacqueline de Decker, Father Gorrée and Mr John J. McGee, for sending me precious data and information.

To Mother Teresa I cannot express adequately my gratitude for being privileged to collaborate with her, even if in an humble manner, in the spiritual formation of hundreds of devoted Sisters who daily spread God's love in the six continents.

When I told Mother Teresa that I had finished writing this book, she made a single comment which sums up her spirit and attitude: 'If this book causes a single person to make one act of love for God, it was worth all the trouble and labour of writing it'.

Thank you, Mother.

Sacred Heart Church
3 Lenin Sarani
Calcutta — 700 013

1. Father, Tell Them

'I heard a voice behind me shouting like a trumpet; 'Write down all that
you see in a book, and send it to the seven churches.'
(*Rev. 1, 10–11*)

'I want to see you', said Mother Teresa. 'I must talk to you.'

She was just back from Mexico where, as a Vatican Delegate at
the International Women's Conference, she had spoken on
woman's role in society. She led some eighty American tourists
into the courtyard of the mother-house. I was delighted at the
prospect of meeting her again.

We entered the courtyard, followed by the tourists. The Indian lady serving as official guide to the tourists approached
Mother Teresa and asked her: 'Would you kindly address them,
they would like to hear a few words about your work.' Mother
agreed.

First she was made to pay the price of celebrity: as she stood
before the crowd, cameras clicked. After this Mother sat down
on the cement floor of the courtyard. Some tourists followed her
example; others stood in a semi-circle. In a corner of the courtyard, Sisters were filling buckets of water from a hand pump. In
a class-room others were studying. From the chapel came the
sound of voices singing psalms to the praise of the Lord. Mother
very simply spoke of the work of the Sisters and of the love for
Jesus that prompted them; of the poor who were so patient and
kind and joyful; of crippled children whom she had befriended
and knew by name. She spoke of God and of the happiness of serving him in the poor, with simplicity, humility, homeliness. This
was an echo of the Sermon on the Mount. The Gospel came
alive: Blessed are you the poor, and you the patient, and you,
eager to listen to one who speaks of God.

When she was free, Mother Teresa returned to the tiny parlour

where ministers, cardinals and bishops have sat on simple
wooden chairs before a small table, talking to one of our
generation's great spiritual energizers. On the wall, charts spelled
out the aims, activities and location of the Missionaries of Charity, the religious congregation she founded.

'How was Mexico, Mother?' I asked.

'Too much politics,' she answered. 'Disappointing. They did
not mention God.'

She added, for fear of being unfair to anyone: 'Maybe someone
did, but I did not hear the name of God mentioned.' No doubt,
God's name would have rung a bell in her heart.

'This is rather strange,' I said, 'considering that many important Moslem ladies were present at the meeting.'

'I spoke of the dignity of women,' she continued, 'of their
God-given functions and prerogatives. As mothers, as wives,
they are called to be the heart of the home, to make a happy
home for their husbands and children. What a noble calling, to
be the mothers of the human race. I told them it was their
privilege to give generously, as God himself gives to his
children.'

'Did the President of Mexico call you to the Palace?'

'Yes, he wants us to start a house in Mexico itself. At the Palace
I met the President, his wife and three of their eight children. I
spoke of our work and of the love of Jesus. When I spoke of
Jesus, his wife was crying.'

'Yes, of course, women are more sensitive to religion than
men.'

'No, it is not so. The President is deep. He gave me the impression of being very deep. He insisted on our coming without
delay. He said he would give us a house and see to the travel expenses of the Sisters. I must send him some of my best Sisters. I
told him that as religious we require the permission of the Cardinal to establish a house in his archdiocese. This should not be
difficult, since the Cardinal had already asked us to come to
Mexico.

'I think the civil and religious powers do not collaborate much
there. I had an excellent occasion of bringing them together. The
President himself contacted the Cardinal and gave me his authorisation to start a house in Mexico. I hope to return there in
October with some Sisters and to start work without delay.'

Speed is typical of Mother Teresa. At times she opens a house a few weeks after the official request has been made. As Superior General, she has to refer to no one, to ask nobody's permission. Later that will change, as the Institute continues to increase in numbers.

'From Mexico I went to Lima, Peru, where we have recently opened a house; then to New York, to London, Rome, and back here.'

'What was Lima like?'

'Latin America offers tremendous opportunities for religious work. It is mainly religious help that is asked of us there. The people are short of priests and nuns. My Sisters must do all that priests normally do, except say Mass and hear confessions. In practice they are like deacons. Take the case of marriages: the Sisters make all preparatory arrangements and have the marriages celebrated. In one place they had thirty marriages celebrated together. In another village they regularized the unions of three generations of couples living together: grandparents, parents and children. A lawyer works with them to arrange for the civil marriages — he gives his time free. When they have received the sacrament of matrimony, the couples are so happy.

'Splendid, Mother. You require more Sisters to do God's work over there. I hear you have received a large number of applications from girls wanting to join the Institute?'

'Yes, I have received of late fifty applications from girls who wish to join us, from America, Australia, England, Africa. We have some very good postulants in Africa. One Japanese girl has applied, though we have as yet no house in Japan.'

'We have three novitiates: in Calcutta, Melbourne, Rome. Altogether at present we have two hundred and nine novices. Most of them are in Calcutta.'

'Why do they join you, what brings them to you?'

'I have received a sheaf of beautiful letters from candidates from Europe and America. The girls say they want a life of prayer, a life of poverty, humility, in the following of Jesus. Is that not wonderful? And this happens at a time when others complain of a lack of vocations and say that the youth of today are not ready for a life of humility, poverty, and obedience. I find nothing of the sort. Ask them to do something hard for Jesus, and they will come forward.

'We require many more Sisters. I have fifty-eight applications
for new houses. I cannot take them all. The Archbishop of
Trinidad asked me for a house. We have recently opened one in
Papua. The Sisters had to look on the map to find out where that
country is. The Bishop is extremely poor; he cannot help much.
But I thought it was one more reason for us to go to his help.'

Fifty-eight houses asked for: as Mother puts seven or eight
Sisters in each house, that would mean about 450 Sisters just to
start these houses. She has 209 novices in the two years novitiate,
which allows her to dispose of about a hundred Sisters a year at
present. The Congregation is young, and the mortality rate is
very low; few die, and not many leave after their first vows.
Still, it would require about five years to comply with all the
requests; and many more will be coming meanwhile. The
backlog of applications will go on increasing, unless the recruitment can be much accelerated, which seems highly probable.

Then I presented my own request:

'Mother, I have to ask you a favour; may I write a book on
you and the Missionaries of Charity? Will you allow me to do
so? We have worked many years together. I intend to write from
the spiritual angle, to show your motivation, the hand of God
directing and protecting your Congregations.'

'Yes, Father, write about us. You have known us well, you
have been with us from the beginning. We have the same ideas.'

'You must have our Constitutions. But mainly, you must tell
people what brings us here. Tell them,' said Mother, and she
became eloquent, pleading, passionately involved – 'tell them
that we are not here for the work, we are here for Jesus. All we
do is for Him. We are first of all religious; we are not social
workers, not teachers, not nurses or doctors, we are religious
Sisters. We serve Jesus in the poor. We nurse Him, feed Him,
clothe Him, visit Him, comfort Him in the poor, the abandoned,
the sick, the orphans, the dying. But all we do, our prayer, our
work, our suffering is for Jesus. Our life has no other reason or
motivation. This is a point many people do not understand. I
serve Jesus twenty-four hours a day, whatever I do is for Him.
And He gives me strength. I love Him in the poor and the poor
in Him. But always the Lord comes first.

'Whenever a visitor comes to this house, I take him to the
chapel to pray for a while. I tell him: "Let us first greet the

Master of the house. Jesus is here; it is for Him we work, to Him we devote ourselves. He gives us the strength to carry on this life and to do so with happiness. Without Him we could not do what we do; we certainly could not continue doing it for a whole life-time. One year, two years, perhaps; but not during a whole life, without thought of reward, without expectation of anything good except to suffer with Him who loved us so much that He gave His life for us. Without Jesus our life would be meaningless, incomprehensible; Jesus explains our life.'

Mother Teresa took a deep breath, then summed up her briefing with a strong command: 'Father, tell them, WE DO IT FOR JESUS.'

As I walked home, the thought struck me: She is Paul writing to the Colossians: 'There is only Christ: He is everything and he is in everything.' (Col. 1, 11) And Mother Teresa's command rang in my ears: 'Tell them: we do it for Jesus.'

2. The Call

'One day ... the Holy Spirit said, 'I want Barnabas and Saul set apart
for the work to which I have called them.'

(*Acts 13, 2–3*)

Father Henry Speaks
Father Julien Henry received me in his small office at St Teresa's
church presbytery. This room was so crowded with boxes,
books, gadgets and instruments that there was not even a chair in
it and we both had to stand for one hour. He usually writes at a
high desk, standing. I asked him:
'Father Henry, you have known Mother Teresa longer and
better than anyone else. What struck you most in her? What
would you say is her main quality? Why did she succeed to such
an extent?'
Father Henry reflected silently, as if lost in prayer. Then he
answered slowly, with deep feeling and emotion.
'What is most extraordinary is the enormous amount of good
Almighty God has worked through this humble instrument. God
has used this woman with all her qualities and defects, yes, her
great qualities and her defects, with her weak training, to do His
work, because she is completely subservient to Him. She obeys
His promptings, His direction, without questioning. She does not
think of herself, she does everything for Him. And she does it
with such complete trust in His power that nothing seems impossible to her. It is all done for God.
'In all her interviews, even with unbelievers, even with non-
Christians, she insists that what she and the Sisters do is for God,
for our Lord Jesus Christ. All they do is for Christ; and they find
in their love for Jesus, in prayer and in adoration of the Blessed
Eucharist the strength to serve the poor.
'She comes from peasant stock and from a community of hill

people. An Albanian from Yugoslavia, she is tough and a revolutionary. If the structures stand in the way of fulfilling your ideas, change them, destroy them, ignore them – that is what happened in her case.

'God made use of her spiritual and human qualities and weaknesses to produce extraordinary fruits. In His hands she has been supple. He guides her. Her ideas came gradually, her aim became clearer and clearer, until one day it was concretised in a deep spiritual experience in the train taking her to Darjeeling.

'In those days she was educating Bengali girls at St Mary's High School, Entally. She was very insistent about their spiritual training, as was also Mother Cenacle, her companion.

'We must remember what had brought Mother Teresa to India. As a school-girl, Agnes, as she was then called, was caught in the wave of enthusiasm for the missions and for the expansion of the Kingdom of Christ, a truly spiritual Kingdom "not of this world", and for the work of spreading the Gospel in the missions, an enthusiasm generated by the writings of Pope Pius XI and highlighted by the institution of the Feast of Christ the King.'

In the Sodality she prayed and meditated on these ideas; she became aflame with the desire of spending herself for the cause of Christ, for the Gospel that was to be preached to all men.

'And so,' continued Father Henry, 'through the paper of the Sodality of Our Lady, Agnes learnt about the Indian Missions. Some Yugoslav Jesuits who had recently come to Bengal worked in the Ganges Delta, South of Calcutta.

Anthony, whilst studying theology at St Mary's College at Kurseong, in the Himalayas, regularly despatched news of the Bengal mission and of the work among the Nepalis of the Darjeeling District. He sent hundreds of letters to friends in Yugoslavia and elsewhere.

'So,' continued Father Henry, 'Agnes learned of the religious, educational and charitable work carried on by missionaries in Bengal. She decided to consecrate her life to this apostolate and enquired about the means of going to India. She was advised to seek admission into the Congregation of the Loreto Nuns who worked in Bengal. Their headquarters were in Dublin. Agnes would have to join them, learn English, and ask to be sent to the missions. She did so.'

When she arrived in India in January 1929 she was sent to the novitiate at Darjeeling, in the Himalayas, where the very scenery speaks of God's majesty, power and beauty.

'At the end of her two years of novitiate she took her first vows of religion. She was then attached to the High School for Bengali girls run by the Loreto nuns at Entally, on Calcutta's Eastern side. There for some twenty years she taught geography and history; later she became Headmistress. She was also put in charge of the Daughters of St Anne, a diocesan Congregation of Indian Sisters, who wore a blue saree and taught in the Bengali secondary school.

'The Loreto nuns at Entally occupy a large property purchased with the money bequeathed to them by a wealthy Protestant planter. In this spacious property the Sisters run an English high school for over five hundred girls, boarders, including a large number of orphans who pay no fees whatever. In the same property the Bengali high school houses two to three hundred boarders and some day scholars, mostly from families of modest means.

'The Loreto nuns are well known for their college and six high schools in Calcutta. They are generally esteemed and respected as hard working religious and as first rate educators. At Entally, Mother Teresa devoted herself whole-heartedly to the intellectual and spiritual formation of Bengali girls under the direction of Mother Cenacle, a Loreto nun from Mauritius, a saintly person.

'At Entally there was a Sodality of the Blessed Virgin for the girls, where they imbibed the same ideas that had brought Mother Teresa to India.'

'You were the spiritual director of that Sodality, Father Henry?'

'Yes. Besides the spiritual meetings there was a study club to which Hindu girls also asked to be admitted. Then we had various activities. Every week a group visited the Nilratan Sarkar Hospital. We rotated the girls so as to have some continuity in the apostolate. We first sent numbers one, two, three; the next week numbers two, three, four; then numbers three, four, five and so on. The girls grew enthusiastic about this work, which was mainly religious: consoling the patients, cheering them up, rendering them small services, writing letters for them. Another group went to visit the slums. Behind the wall of the school there was the slum of Motijhil. The girls went to do service there. Mother herself never went with them.

'Mother saw the dire poverty of many people in and around Calcutta. She felt an inner prompting to do something to relieve the hardships of the very poor, and to lead them to God. Spiritually they were completely neglected – truly sheep without a shepherd. She realized that within the structures of organized education, aimed mainly at the middle classes, in which she worked, it would be impossible to achieve this aim. She had to get out of the system and start something quite different.

'At the same time, some of the girls she was teaching and who visited the poor in the slums and the sick in hospital, expressed to her the desire of becoming nuns so that they could devote themselves fully to the apostolate among the very poor.'

Then came God's call. 'It was,' Mother Teresa told me 'on the tenth of September, 1946, in the train that took me to Darjeeling, the hill station in the Himalayas, that I heard the call of God.' In quiet, intimate prayer with her Lord, she heard distinctly what she says was for her, 'a call within a call.' 'The message,' she explains, 'was quite clear: I was to leave the convent and help the poor whilst living among them. It was an order. I knew where I belonged, but I did not know how to get there.'

She had already been called by God to the religious life and there was never any question of abandoning it. God was calling her to another kind of work and service in the religious life.

Mother felt intensely that Jesus wanted her to serve him in the poorest of the poor, the uncared for, the slum-dwellers, the abandoned, the homeless. Jesus invited her to serve him and follow him in actual poverty, material poverty, to practise a style of life that would make her similar to the needy in whom he was present, suffered and loved.

As at the Annunciation Mary Immaculate had answered 'Yes, be it done to me according to your word, according to God's will,' so, whole-heartedly, to this call of God she heard in her heart, Mother Mary Teresa answered 'Yes.' She did not know how it would be done, but she surrendered to God in unlimited faith.

It was a flash of light on the road to Damascus, a meeting with

Jesus, injecting a new spirit and direction to her apostolic life. This light did not blind her — she was prepared for it, accustomed as she was to follow God's inspiration and having reflected as she had on the unfortunate lot of so many who had little chance of knowing God's infinite love for them. Mother accepted. There was no encounter, no struggle, no compulsion: obediently, lovingly, she accepted. Was she not wedded to Jesus, ready to follow him in utter poverty? Did she not always trust him and do His will fully

The Missionaries of Charity keep this day as 'Inspiration Day,' for truly it was the start of their Institute.

As the Apostles had been prepared by Christ for the final call, not only to discipleship, but to be apostles, so, says Father Henry, 'Mother Teresa had been prepared.'

In the train, the inspiration or call was crystallized, became a clear and definite expression of God's will. This 'call within a call' originating from God resembled that of Barnabas and Paul.

'One day,' say the *Acts*, 'while they were offering worship to the Lord and keeping a fast, the Holy Spirit said, "I want Barnabas and Saul set apart for the work to which I have called them." So it was that after fasting and prayer they laid their hands on them and sent them off.' (*Acts 13, 2–3*) The Christian community, aware that the call came from the Holy Spirit, sent them off cheerfully, with prayers and their blessing. In these days, more distant from Pentecost, the Holy Spirit's call came to a nun who would have to reveal it to the authorities of the Church, the Archbishop of Calcutta and her Superiors, and obtain their approval and blessing.

On her return to Calcutta, Mother Teresa made her desires known to some members of her community, who listened to her, as may be expected, with mixed feelings.

'When he had become very old and retired to St Xaviers' College, Archbishop Périer said to me,' recalled Father Henry, ' "One day, as I was making the visit of Entally Convent, someone told me that a young nun of the community had some queer ideas. Now, whenever anyone tried to put me on my guard in this way, I always asked myself whether the Hand of God might not be there, and gave full freedom to the person to explain his or her case. If the religious is humble, obedient, dutiful, the impulse may come from God." '

The Archbishop applied St Paul's advice to test the various spirits to find out if they come from God. He gave the young nun with strange ideas a sympathetic hearing as she outlined her plan to work among the poorest and most needy. Of course, to realize her plans she would have to leave her religious Congregation and start a new one.

After speaking to the Archbishop of her plans, she was transferred to Asansol for reasons of health. But the Archbishop insisted with her Superior that she be brought back to Calcutta, since she had applied to him for permission to leave the convent for a time. Meanwhile, trouble arose in the school, fanned by the political situation of the day. The school authorities could not settle the dispute with the girls. When Mother Teresa returned to Entally, she called the girl leaders and within half an hour the trouble was over. They could not resist her appeals to sanity.

The magnetic influence she exerted was to be the trump card which helped her to fulfill her desire to start her new congregation.

Many years later, I asked Mother:
'Did the Archbishop ever ask you for a sign from God?'
'No, he did not ask me for a sign.'
'Did you give him one?'
'No, I did not give him any.'
Had the Archbishop done so, he would have set the matter immediately in a spiritual and supernatural context. A superior may do this. A religious who seems specially able to perform a task at home, when he requests to be sent to the missions, may be told by his superior: 'Give me a sign that God wants you to go to the missions.' The religious then convinces his superior somehow.

But in the case of Mother Teresa things did not go so far. The religious authority tried to discover whether Mother's vocation to a special work was not an illusion, but was true and had chances of success. Some indications convinced the Archbishop that the Finger of God might be there.

The first difficulty was political, and arose from the atmosphere and the mentality prevailing in the days preceding and following the Independence of India.

'One day,' said Father Henry, 'the Archbishop asked me

"What would you think of a European woman who dressed in Indian style and went out to work among the very poor in the slums, at the head of a group of Bengali girls? Would she succeed? Would she be accepted?" ' The point was: in those days of acute nationalistic feelings, what would be the reaction of the thinking public? This was before India became independent, when under the inspiration of Gandhiji groups of congressmen went out to do social service among the poorer classes.

'I answered the Archbishop: "Undoubtedly this is a gamble: there is a real risk of arousing opposition. But it could be tried, especially if you have the right person. She will have to make herself acceptable to the civic and political leaders. With the poor, the matter presents less difficulty – they will be won over by the charity of the person who bends over their misery, whatever her nationality.

'And so, the Archbishop agreed to try the gamble and give Mother Teresa a chance.'

The second difficulty was that Rome did not favour an unnecessary multiplication of religious institutes of women. There existed already too many small ones. A bishop who applied for the approbation of a new religious institute in his diocese had to show that none of the existing ones could do the particular work for which the new one was established. Now, Calcutta Archdiocese already had a religious congregation, the Daughters of St Anne, under the jurisdiction of the Archbishop. They devoted themselves to the care and education of the poor in the villages and in Calcutta. They dressed in Indian style, slept in a dormitory, ate very simple food, lived in the Indian manner, spoke Bengali, worked among the poor and unsophisticated.

The Archbishop would have liked Mother Teresa to first try to work out her plans with their help and collaboration. But Mother quickly found that she could not. The sisters had their tradition, their own activities, their ways of proceeding. She wanted a group that would be highly mobile, that would visit the people, that would work not only among the poor, but among the poorest of the poor. She could not simply follow in others' footsteps. She wanted to start from scratch, train her novices in her own way, make them imbibe her own spirit. The future was to prove her right.

The Daughters of St Anne lived in the same compound as

Mother and worked in the school of St Mary's where Mother Teresa had been headmistress. They were understandably worried about their future prospects and asked me, as I was then their spiritual adviser, to speak to them on the consequences of this new religious institute that would compete with them for the few Bengali girls who wished to enter the religious life. I told them that this was a challenge to them. . . .

Indeed they have multiplied, and their Congregation has increased in strength, initiative, the variety of works undertaken, in self-reliance. They now have their own Mother General; they run their own schools and orphanages very successfully. Competition has proved to be an excellent stimulus.

It took some time and much discussion and prayer for light before the Archbishop was ready to apply to Rome for permission to start in his archdiocese a new religious Congregation for women. At least ten novices had to join Mother. Constitutions would have to be drafted and sent to Rome for approval. The first step was to obtain from Rome exclaustration or permission for a religious, bound by perpetual vows, to live for a time outside a convent and to be no longer under religious Superiors, but directly under the authority of the Bishop.

Mother Teresa's request for exclaustration was duly despatched to Rome, in February 1948. When the permission arrived, Mother prepared to leave.

'Did you have any difficulties with your religious Superiors before you left?' I asked her at the time of the Jubilee.

'None whatever.' she answered, 'they were most understanding and cooperative.'

And so Mother Teresa, in response to God's call, on the 16th of August 1948 walked out of the convent, closed the door behind her and found herself on a Calcutta street, alone, in the dark.

God had called her to himself in a very special way. Twenty-seven years later, Mother confided to me:

'To leave Loreto was my greatest sacrifice, the most difficult thing I have ever done. It was much more difficult than to leave my family and country to enter religious life. Loreto meant everything to me.

'In Loreto I had received my spiritual training; I had become a religious there. I had given myself to Jesus in the Institute. I liked the work, teaching the girls.'

As an adolescent Agnes had been called by God and had turned to him. Following His call, she left her family, her father's house, her culture, her country, all she had been accustomed to see, to hear and to love, to go to a foreign land. In the first flush of youthful enthusiasm and generosity it was not too difficult. But the first period of training would exact more self-denial.

Then, gradually God was to invite her to a more complete donation of herself, a second turning towards Him in deeper faith and a more intense yearning to do only what pleases Him. This grace must have come after some years of religious life, when she had acquired the habit of doing the difficult thing for God, of choosing to carry the Cross with Jesus, of thinking only of the Beloved, until she saw the world in God and God in the world. This grace is given or offered to many a person faithful to God's grace and ready for great sacrifices.

One day, she received from God a special invitation. Some chosen souls are granted a great grace, which may be offered once or twice only; if they accept it, they start on the road to holiness.

God bestows this grace upon those He finds sufficiently generous, and on whom He had special designs, whom He wishes to entrust with a special mission or task, who have the mettle and the will to accept suffering in His service and for His glory.

Masters of spirituality describe the soul's progress: it turns to God in a more intense, complete, thorough manner, after a heroic self-surrender, in response to a powerful grace, which invites and strengthens the soul.

Mother went through this spiritual experience.

'It was much more difficult than leaving my family when I entered the convent. Yes, when I left the convent I did not run away from it to obtain more freedom.'

She left the security of the convent, its friendliness, its way of life, its spiritual help, in order to throw herself blindly into God's hands, in pure faith, not asking, not knowing, not questioning, but blindly surrendering to God's guidance.

She was on the street, with no shelter, no company, no helper no money, no employment, no promise, no guarantee, no security.

'My God, you, only you. I trust in your call, your inspiration; you will not let me down.' Now, she was His.

Patna

After the break with her past way of life, a period of training afforded a welcome period of transition and reflection. Mother Teresa left Calcutta and proceeded to Patna for a short course in nursing and outdoor dispensary work under the guidance of the Medical Missionary Sisters of Mother Dengel. To be of service to the poor, she had to know, therefore she had to learn.

At Patna, on the bank of the Ganges, the medical Missionary Sisters run an efficient hospital to which is attached a popular and well attended outdoor department. The Sisters also direct an excellent nurses' training course.

In July 1969, as a patient in the hospital's surgical department, I enquired about the Calcutta student Sister. She was still remembered as a keen student who had packed as much knowledge and experience into her three or four month's stay as anyone could acquire in so short a time.

At Patna Mother Teresa also sustained the first shock and upset to her plans and ideas concerning the way of life she and the girls she expected to join her would embrace. She had intended to live in utter poverty — they would live, dress and eat like the very poor among whom they would work, in an effort to bring them to God, and whom they would serve as the suffering members of Christ.

Mother Dengel, an Austrian-born woman of unlimited zeal and energy, had obtained from the Holy See the permission for her nuns to practise both surgery and midwifery in hospitals run by them, something new in the Catholic Church. Thus, she could understand and sympathize with a nun wishing to start new ways and activities in religious life.

Mother Teresa explained to Mother Dengel and her Sisters that she planned to start a congregation whose members would live like the poor in India. The nuns' diet would not even consist of simple rice and pulses, which is modest enough, but would be just 'rice and salt' a diet considered to be below the poverty line, the humblest of Bengali diets.

'We shall eat rice and salt,' said Mother Teresa with determination.

'If you make your Sisters do that,' retorted Mother Dengel, emphatically, 'you will commit a serious sin. Within a short time those young girls will fall a prey to tuberculosis and die. How do you want your Sisters to work, if their bodies receive no sustenance? The very poor work very little, become sick and die young. Do you want your nuns to suffer that fate? Or do you wish them to be strong and able to labour for Christ?'

Mother Teresa accepted this expert advice. She could not tempt God, could not ask His divine Providence to go continually against the laws of nature He had established, and work a continual miracle for the health of her Sisters, when food was available. Humbly she changed her plans. The Sisters would receive the sustenance their bodies required, their food would be simple, without luxury; obediently they would eat the portion they were given.'

Years later, Mother told me: 'The Medical Missionaries of Patna said I was to feed my Sisters well; I have followed their advice.'

Indeed, years ago several Indian Bishops had trouble with poorly fed nuns and seminarians who suffered from tuberculosis and other diseases. The Bishops took adequate measures and among the younger generation the trouble is over.

The good Lord was training His loving spouse, correcting here and there, moderating where need be what might have been otherwise excessive zeal. Mother's Sisters could not all be expected to receive the same charisms and grace God had granted her with such lavishness.

At Patna Holy Family Hospital, Mother met Miss Jacqueline de Decker to whom she revealed her plans. This young Belgian woman would have liked to join the future Institute. But her physical condition would not allow it. She was later to become one of Mother's 'Second Selves' and to organize the wing of the Sick and Suffering who would pray and suffer for the success of the Institute and its apostolate.

And in this hospital Mother later lost her first religious, who left earth for heaven. One of her novices died there, after taking her religious vows on her death-bed, the first fruits the Congregation offered to its Lord.

The short stay at Patna was soon over – an interlude in the

drama. Like her Master coming out of the wilderness after preparing Himself for His public life by prayer and fasting, Mother Teresa was ready to begin the task the Father had appointed her to perform for the glory of His Son. She returned to Calcutta, where she found a temporary shelter with the Little Sisters of the poor.

First Beginnings

'One day in December 1948,' said Father Henry, 'on her return from Patna, Mother appeared at St Teresa's presbytery dressed in a white saree with a blue border.'

'Do you recognize me?' she asked me.

'Of course, Mother Teresa.'

'Where is Motijhil?'

'What? You don't know? Just behind the wall of the school where you were teaching.'

I asked a woman to show her the way. They went together. Soon I heard that Mother had found a vacant room in the slum.

'What rent?' she asked.

'Five rupees per month,' said the owner.

'I'll take it,' she said.

'The next day,' continued Father Henry, 'as I was passing through Motijhil, a very poor slum area, where we had some Catholics, I heard a voice repeating the first letters of the Bengali alphabet. I looked inside the room and what do I see? Mother Teresa teaching a few children. No table, no chair, no blackboard, no chalk. With a stick she drew figures on the earth.'

After that she went to see the Corporation scavengers in their quarters, enquiring about their families, the sick, the children.

At night she stayed at St Joseph's Home, run by the Little Sisters of the Poor for Aged Persons without means or relatives able to support them. It is one hour's walk from Motijhil.

Jeanne Jugan, the French nun who started the Congregation of the Little Sisters of the Poor had much in common with Mother Teresa. She insisted on absolute poverty – the houses of the Institute were to have no foundations, no regular income, not even a bank account. The Sisters went out and still go out daily on a begging mission to obtain the support needed for their inmates.

The spirituality of the Little Sisters is centred on humility and charity, a delicate, refined, exquisite, perfect charity. There lived in the house a Sister who for forty years remained in charge of the kitchen – a wonderful soul, a true mystic who would tell her confessor 'I love Our Lord to the point of madness.' To Him she had given everything, and Our Lord as usual had asked her much.

The Sisters looked after some two hundred old people who had no resources. Mother Teresa lived in that holy house for a short time. God, who had called her, would soon show that she was His chosen one.

Motijhil, the first small school
Right at the beginning, when she was still alone, Mother took me round to show me her work, as she would do with many visitors later on.

We went along by the dwellings of the Corporation sweepers, crossed some railway lines, walked through a slum area. No one seemed to notice her, no one greeted her or gave any sign of recognition. She was not yet part of their life. We looked inside a mud hut.

'This is our school room,' said Mother Teresa.

'How many pupils do you have?'

'Thirty-five,' I think she said, 'when they are all present. But usually some are sick or absent for some reason or other.

'I teach them the alphabet; and also how to wash and comb their hair. I give them a cake of soap as prize for regularity, attention and cleanliness.'

I thought they would prefer sweets, but made no comment.

'Then they receive milk at midday.'

She was taking the wrong person round; as a professor of economics, who knew how to obtain the maximum results from our limited resources, I could not be impressed. The whole thing was rather pathetic and inefficient. Here was the headmistress of a fairly good high school trying to teach the alphabet to children who would never become literate, and teaching the use of soap to children who would not be able to afford to buy it.

She was making a desperate effort to uplift the very poor, to give them a sense of respectability and teach them that God loves

them. Unless she could gather a team around her, these efforts
would produce no fruits. But would anyone join her for this
task? Or would she find some other means of helping the sufferers of mankind?

'This is not much,' she commented.

But we, who were doing more pleasant work, gave her all encouragement.

These were the pathetic days of the small entries in the diary
she then kept. Years later she showed it to me. There were no
special secrets, no revelations, just small notes on the persons she
had met or on some particular happening. Some of them remained embedded in my memory twenty-five years later.

'Met N., who said there was nothing to eat at home. I gave
him the fare for my tram, all the money I had, and walked
home.'

At the time of the Jubilee, I reminded Mother of the small
notebook and asked if she still had it. She shrugged her shoulders
and said: 'No, I think I threw it away.' The right thing to do.

Meanwhile God was training her – she had to feel utterly
useless, inadequate to the task. She had to cling to Him, throw
herself entirely on Him: 'You, Lord, only you, all for you; make
use of me.

'You pulled me out of my convent where I was useful. Now
guide me, as you wish.'

The Lord heard; He took over. He got her a house, He sent
her helpers. She was to become the leader of a team that would
extend her in time and space, as she extended Christ Himself. Her
first great task would be to build and train her team.

3. The Upper Room

'Listen, said Jesus, as you go into the city you will meet a man carrying a pitcher of water. Follow him into the house he enters and tell the owner of the house, 'The Master asks: Where is the dining room in which I can eat the passover with my disciples? The man will show you a large upper room furnished with couches. Make the preparations there.'

(Luke 22, 10–12)

Michael Gomes speaks
'Brother Michael, tell me all you remember about Mother Teresa during her stay in your house.'

I called him Brother, because for many years we had worked together in the Legion of Mary. We were sitting in one of the rooms occupied by Mother Teresa in his family's three-storeyed house.

'Willingly, Father. But first I must repeat what I said some time ago. The Chairman of a group of Co-Workers of the Missionaries of Charity praised me saying "We are happy to have today in our midst the man who did so much for Mother Teresa, by putting her up free of charge in his own house and giving her his time and all possible help." I answered:

'Friends, it is we who have been benefited. If we have given much, we have received much more in return. Mother Teresa's presence in our family house has been a wonderful source of blessing.

'Mother,' he continued, 'occupied the second floor. From the ground floor the staircase leads to the top floor directly into the room the Sisters used as chapel. The wooden altar and wooden candlesticks and furnishings were made by Father Henry with the help of his boys. Above the altar hung the picture of the Immaculate Heart of Mary given by Father Van Exem, who was then the rector of the church of Our Lady of Dolours. It is now in the chapel of the Mother-house.

'Archbishop Périer came several times to say Mass for the Sisters during the first years. Cardinal Spellman also came to see Mother in this house.'

'How did it happen that she came to your house?'

'Well, Father, we were four brothers living in this house. At the time of the partition of India, two of my brothers opted for East Pakistan, now Bangladesh. Two of us stayed in Calcutta.

'One day Father Van Exem came to our house and asked me "Could you find some place for Mother Teresa to stay; a mud house, a hut, something simple, anything, but close by. Can you find something?"

'Then came the voice of a child. My daughter, aged eight, said: "Daddy, the rooms upstairs are empty; there is nobody. Mother could come here."

"No," said Father Van Exem "that is far too good, it is not what she wants. She wants something much more humble."

'But we insisted, "Father, send her here. She is a nun, she must be treated well. She does the work of God." And so in February 1949 Mother came and occupied the second floor.

'Was she alone?'

'No, she came with a woman who served at St Mary's School, Charur Ma, a widow.'

'Mother took my eight-year-old daughter to visit the slums with her. Then, she needed medicines. So I went out to beg for medicines with her.

'Once we went to a big shop with a list of medicines she required. The manager was very busy. Mother showed her written list and asked for them all free.

' "You come to the wrong place, lady" answered the manager. "Let me finish my work in peace."

'Mother and I sat down. She said her rosary. When she had finished, the manager said: "All right, here are three parcels with the medicines you need. You may have them as a gift from the Company." '

In March 1949, on the Feast of St Joseph, there was a knock at Mother's door. She opened it and stood motionless, whilst her heart beat faster, faster, as she looked at the frail figure facing her, and heard her say: 'Mother, I have come to join you.'

'It will be a hard life; are you prepared for it?'

'I know it will be hard; I am prepared for it.' And the girl stepped in.

Mother turned to her Lord, in gratitude: 'Dear Jesus, how good You are. So You are sending them! You keep the promise You made me. Lord Jesus, thank You for your goodness.'

The first candidate to join Mother Teresa became Sister Agnes, taking Mother's baptismal name.

At her evening prayers Mother Teresa poured out her heart in thanksgiving and expressed her joy and confidence in God who protected her and blessed her in this manner. Now, they would start work.

I did not ask Mother what her reaction had been; I did not need to. I experienced the same feelings when the first of my ex-students told me: 'I want to become a Christian.' I also asked him: 'Do you realize that it will be terribly hard for you? Have you the courage to do it?'

'I have the courage' he answered.

'Dear Lord, thank You' I prayed. So, in spite of all they told me — that I had false hopes and was wasting my time, that educated people were not ready to embrace Christianity — you have heard my prayers and those of my parents and friends.'

Mother never forgot that Sister Agnes had been the first to believe in 'the Cause' and to trust her inspiration as coming from God. A special relationship was established between the two of them, which everyone respected and understood. They were like Paul and Timothy. Paul had brought Timothy to the faith and appointed him as a Church leader. A special friendship would unite them until death; together they would work for the glory of the Lord Jesus, even when separated physically.

Sister Agnes became Mother's second self; for a time she replaced her as Mistress of Novices; then she was put in charge of the Mother-house and replaced Mother during her frequent absences when new foundations were being established.

Some weeks later, a second candidate appeared, and then a third. With joy Mother could say and write that their numbers were increasing.

In May 1949 Mother writes to a friend in Europe:

'You will be glad to hear that at present I have got three companions — great and zealous workers. We have five different slums where we go for a few hours. What suffering; what want of God. And yet, we are so few to carry Our Lord among them. You should see their eager faces, how they brighten up when the Sisters come. Dirty and naked though they be, their hearts are full of affection. I trust in your prayers. Ask Our Lady also to give more Sisters. In Calcutta itself, we could have full work even if we were twenty.'

And so they were four. Six months later Mother could report that they were five: a slow increase. As for work, what were even twenty Sisters among Calcutta's six or seven million people? Mother did not seem to foresee that one day they would be not twenty, but two hundred, and still unable to cope with the task.

In November 1947 she writes:

'Pray much that the little Society may grow in sanctity and members if it is the will of God. Yes, there is so much to be done; at present we are five. But, please God, more will join, and then we will be able to make a ring of charity round Calcutta, using our centres in the different slums as points from whence the love of Our Lord may freely radiate on the great city of Calcutta.'

Here she expresses her aim clearly to a person able to understand and share her life's goal to make Jesus known and loved by the poorest of the poor.

She succeeds in bringing children to church on Sundays; she writes:

'You will be glad to know that at Boitakhana we have a Sunday Mass for poor slum children. We bring the poor children and their mothers to church. We have up to 120 mothers and 300 children. We started last May with twenty-six children only'

Already Mother has obtained the active collaboration of many lay people whose devotion she praises:

'At the dispensary the Catholic doctors and nurses are wonderful. The way they look after the people, you would think they were the princes of the country. Their charity is most wonderful.'

Mother adds a charming note: 'In the slums you can now hear the children sing. Their little faces smile when the Sisters come. And their parents too do not ill-treat their children. This is just what I have been longing to see among the poor. Thank God for all.'

A year after she had found a haven of peace and love at 14 Creek Lane, Mother could rejoice that the Lord had sent her six disciples. In 1950 she writes to her friend in Europe:
'You will be glad to know that we are now seven, and in a few days we shall be eight. Our little chapel was blessed on the 18th December. The work is slowly forming. Ask our Lord to help me to realize His plan.'

Michael Gomes recalls how the group increased and multiplied according to the promise God had made Abraham, the Man of Faith, whom Mother Teresa had imitated in his trust in God:
'The Sisters started coming after a few months. First Sister Agnes. She had been in the school under Mother and she believed in her. Mother never forgot it, Sister Agnes imbibed Mother's spirit. Though very simple and humble, she has always been the second in command, replacing Mother whenever she is out of Calcutta.

'Then came Sister Gertrude, then others, Dorothy, Margaret Mary. This one came from Bangledesh; when she heard Mother had started, nothing could stop her. She knew no English at the time. Many years later she returned to Bangladesh as Superior of the foundation there. She had to organize relief work. She had been well trained. A consignment of good French blankets arrived for distribution to the poor and the refugees. A minister sent his bearer, a bishop sent his driver for a blanket. Sister sent them back empty-handed, saying: "They are for the poor; you are not poor people; you are working men with a decent salary."

'How many Sisters were there when they left?' I asked.
'Thirty or thirty-two.'
Mrs Gomes interposed:
'No, they were exactly twenty-eight.' She was positive about it. She remembered better.
Michael Gomes continued:
'Mother took first one room, then another for the Sisters. Then some got ill, they had to be isolated; Mother asked for a room for the Sisters who were infectious. As the numbers increased, she took the whole floor, and even the annexe.'
'Yes, it has always been like that, she takes all she can get.'

'At first there were only two bathing rooms on their floor. As the number of Sisters started to increase, this created some difficulties, as they had to get ready early. So, Father Henry with some of his boys built some bathing rooms on top of the annexe.

'By eight a.m. the Sisters were all out. They came home for lunch. In the afternoon there was perfect silence in the house. The Sisters had classes, studies and instructions. But after dinner, the house was filled with laughter and singing. The Sisters ran on the terrace; they had tugs-of-war, played and made the whole house tremble. It was good to hear them laugh. After recreation, it was time for prayer and again there was complete silence. They were truly God's children.'

Father Henry recalls that when Mother's first disciples arrived, they expected that the life would be terribly hard and that the food would be insufficient. At their first meal, as Mother put before them a plate well filled with food, they looked at it with astonishment. 'Eat it' said Mother, 'that is your portion.' They were to learn that God wants 'obedience rather than victims'. They had come here to do not their will according to the flesh, but the will of the One who had called them and would send them out – as Christ, who was sent by the Father, said: 'I came to do not my will, but the will of the Father who sent me.'

Father Henry adds; 'In one of my instructions right at the beginning, I told them: "Yes, you have plenty to eat now; food is not lacking. But it may happen that one day on coming home from work you find that there is nothing to eat. . . ." Sister Dorothy interrupted me and said "That day will never come." She had already acquired Mother's trust in God's providence, who looks after his own.'

The house of the Gomes brothers proved to be truly a replica of the Cenacle, the Upper Room in a disciple's house, where Jesus took the Last Supper with His apostles. It was a cenacle hallowed by the presence of the Lord; daily the Last Supper was re-enacted in it and the place remained full of His spirit during the rest of the day.

In this cenacle, the Sisters were, as Jesus had prayed, closely united and acutely conscious of their oneness in the Lord. There they worshipped, prayed, studied, ate, slept, talked, sang and relaxed. There they cooked, washed clothes, scrubbed floors, prepared bandages, mended clothes, There, mainly, they learned the principles and the practice of the spiritual life, of life dedicated to God in union with Jesus. As more novices were admitted, the group grew, took shape, gathered strength.

Mother was Christ in their midst, instructing them, demonstrating to them the purpose of the Institute. They listened, rapt in admiration, full of the desire of giving themselves completely to Jesus. Then, at the end of a full day's work and prayer, they retired to take their rest. Within a few minutes most of the Sisters were fast asleep.

Mother remained working at a small table, writing. She wrote to candidates who wished to join her Institute, to inform them that it would be a hard life; she wrote to priests and to helpers in India and abroad. She drafted some articles of the Constitutions. For a long time she wrote; then, when the task was ended, she joined her hands and slowly fell on her knees to pray to her Lord.

In this atmosphere, close to the living Presence of Christ in the Eucharist, responsible to God for the disciples He had sent her, she summed up the purpose of her coming here as Jesus in His Sacerdotal prayer had summed up the purpose of His coming on earth. With Him she consecrated herself to the Father for the full and perfect sacrifice He wanted of her. With total faith in God's help, protection and goodness, she prayed;

'Father, glorify Your Son that Your Son may return the glory to You; Father, glorify Your Son, let Him be glorified through Your unworthy instruments, for it is for Him, for His glory that we are here, that we work and suffer and pray; all we do is for Jesus; our life has no meaning if it is not all for Him. Let men know Him, and thus come to possess the eternal life He brought us.

'Eternal life, Father, is to know You, the one true God and Jesus Christ, whom You have sent.

'May we bring this eternal life to the poor, deprived as they are of all comfort, of material possessions; may they come to know You, love You, possess You, share in Your life, You who are the God and Father of men and of my Lord Jesus Christ, Source of all truth and goodness and happiness.

'May we bring to You those we meet, those for whom we work, those who help us, those who die in our hands, those we receive as Jesus received the children He blessed, the sick He cured, the sufferers He befriended.

'Father, I pray You for these Sisters, whom You have chosen to serve You and belong to You; they were Yours, and You gave them to me; You want me to lead them to You; You wish them to be an image of Your Son, Your own perfect Image, that men may believe that You have sent Him; that seeing their works, men may acknowledge that Christ was sent by You;

'You gave them to me, and I bring them to You;

'You took them away from the world and its spirit, that they may live in the world as the brides of Jesus, neither belonging to the world nor following its corrupt ways;

'Holy Father, I pray for them that they may be dedicated to Your holy Name, sanctified to You, reserved for Your service, immolated to You in sacrifice. To this end I consecrate myself to You, I dedicate myself as Your victim with Jesus Christ, the Victim of the Sacrifice.'

Father so good, I pray not only for these my Sisters, but for all those who will come to join them and those who through them will be drawn to You and believe in You.

'Father, grant that my Sisters may all be one, as You and Jesus are one; that they may live through Your Spirit.

'That the love with which You loved us may be in them and that Jesus may be in them.'

Mother Teresa let the Spirit pray in her, and asked Him to love her divine Spouse Jesus in her.

Slowly her head fell on her hands. She needed some sleep; tomorrow or perhaps already today there was much work to do for Jesus. She lay down and slept, God's Angel close to the Sisters she was to mould for his service.

They were in the world, but not of the world – they were to keep away from its spirit of greed, pride and sensuality. They wore humble sarees of coarse material, like the poor; from their left shoulder hung a small crucifix. The cross was to be in their life, the cross on their arm, the cross in their heart; the cross calling, teaching, a constant reminder of the cross Christ had carried out of love for men, out of love for them. They were to be for the whole of their life on earth like Paul 'crucified to the world and to whom the world is crucified,' brides of Christ, similar to their divine Spouse.

Mother trained her young Sisters by word and example, as Jesus had done with His apostles at the Last Supper. She told them how they were to treat the poorest of the poor, in whom they were to see Jesus, their Lord and Master, the Son of God become man.

The Gospel recalls how Jesus taught His disciples humble charity.

'As they were at supper, Jesus got up from table, removed His outer garments and, taking a towel, wrapped it round His waist; he then poured water into a basin and began to wash the disciples' feet and to wipe them with the towel He was wearing.' (*John 13, 2–5*) Jesus thus assumes the dress and performs the work of a slave. A Jew could not ask a Jewish servant to wash his feet, he could only ask a slave.

After He had washed his disciples' feet Jesus told them: 'Do you understand what I have done to you? You call me Master and Lord, and rightly; so I am. If I, your Lord and Master, have washed your feet, you should wash each other's feet. I have given you an example so that you may imitate what I have done to you.' And Jesus added: 'Now that you know this, happiness will be yours if you behave accordingly.'

This took place as Jesus was about to institute the Eucharist and give to the world the greatest proof of His love for men. He would not give them spiritual food once only but thousands of times, if they so wished. Similarly He wanted His disciples to perform acts of love and humility not once but many times.

Mother Teresa was teaching her young Sisters to wash the bodies of those in need, to clean their sores and bandage their wounds. They were to do this not a few times, but thousands of times. Their service of love was to last not a few days, not even a year or two, but a whole life, as long as the Lord God wanted them to serve Him in their brothers.

The poor would come to them, emaciated, covered with sores and ulcers, suffering from elephantiasis, venereal disease, cancer, leprosy.

'At times' Mother told me, 'they arrive in a terrible state, filthy, covered with sores, eaten up by syphilis. We wash them all. Of course when a case is really too bad, I do it myself.'

'Of course, Mother.'

Every religious Superior worthy of the name would do so. But it was good to hear it said in all simplicity.

Seeing their Mother doing this, the Sisters also understood what they would be expected to do later, when they would be in charge of a community in some near or distant land.

The sick and the dying would be brought to them. Knowing neither their names, nor their place of origin, nor their antecedents, the Sisters were to treat them all in a loving way.

'It is Christ you tend in the poor,' explained Mother. 'It is His wounds you bathe, His sores you clean, His limbs you bandage. See beyond appearances, hear the words Jesus pronounced long ago; they are still operative today: "What you do to the least of mine you do it to me." When you serve the poor you serve Our Lord Jesus Christ.'

And in the morning, on the way to the slums, the dispensaries, the homes for the dying, the children's homes, the Sisters remembered that it was the Lord they had received in the Eucharist at Mass that they were going to attend, nurse, serve lovingly in His suffering brothers and sisters. They would see Him with the eyes of faith and perform their task with utter respect for Christ present in the poor.

Was it pleasant? It was not; except perhaps for a few who were granted an extraordinary grace. But they did it with faith; they believed in the words of the Lord; 'Now that you know this, happiness will be yours if you behave accordingly.'

They performed their various tasks with cheerfulness, as Mother asked them to. On their way home they might experience the joy the Holy Spirit pours into the hearts of those who belong to God and serve Him only.

Meanwhile Mother was busy writing the Constitutions of the Congregation she wished to found; they were to be sent to Rome for approval.

The structure of the new Institute, its aims and rules had to be determined and approved before the Congregation could start to exist. For this difficult work Father Van Exem's help proved invaluable. He helped Mother to present her case, and defended her plans before the Archbishop.

At the time of the Jubilee, as she remembered the difficult first years, Mother said 'God was good to me, He gave me good

priests to help me in my work: Father Henry, Father Van Exem,'
and she named two others.

Father Celeste Van Exem proved a great help to Mother. He
was a Belgian Jesuit who had been prepared to establish contacts
with Moslems. He had learned Arabic and lived for some time
with the Arab bedouin to imbibe their spirit, assimilate their
language and culture, become acquainted with their religious
life. He came to know Mother Teresa; he espoused her cause and
lent it his support. He greatly helped to frame the Constitutions
of the Missionaries of Charity. He knew Canon Law and could
foresee what might be introduced into the Constitutions and
what would not be allowed by Rome.

Though he supported Mother's ideas, he had to oppose certain
provisions which could not or would not be accepted by the
Roman Congregation for Religious. He spoke for Mother before
the Archbishop; the weight of his knowledge, experience and
perseverance helped her to such an extent that some Sisters called
him 'The Co-Founder' or 'The Cardinal'. Priests would say
jokingly, 'the Cardinal Protector.'

The other priest who helped Mother most was Father Julien
Henry. Father Moyersoen, the Jesuit Superior in Calcutta, had
asked the Belgian Provincial to give him some priests ready to
start work in Bengal immediately. Father Julien Henry offered
his services. Soon he was in Calcutta where he worked for many
years at St Teresa's parish. He may be the man who best knows
Mother, as her spiritual adviser, and who helped most in the
training of her Sisters. He is well informed about the wonderful
saga of love of God and Christian charity for the most needy
enacted by the Missionaries of Charity.

The Constitutions

'Father Henry, who wrote the Constitutions?' I asked him.

'That is a good question,' he answered. 'The first draft of the
constitutions was entirely due to Mother Teresa herself. Her
spiritual background and aspirations are expressed in the
Constitutions she gave to the Missionaries of Charity. You find
in them her passion for the Kingdom of Christ, for preaching the
Gospel and making Christ known and loved by all men; also her
devotion to the Sacred Heart, to Our Lady, to the Blessed

Eucharist and her faithfulness to the Church and to the Pope.

'Father Van Exem helped her, especially with the juridical and organizational aspects of the Constitutions. As a canonist and theologian, he knew what would be acceptable to Rome and what would not. Mother wanted to introduce some measures that were impossible: for example, she did not wish them to own any property, even their own houses. The ownership would have been vested in the Church, which was not possible since the Church of Rome or the Vatican is a foreign body in India.'

St Francis of Assisi had wanted something similar. He did not want to own the houses in which the Friars would live and work, in order to be perfectly poor. But Rome would not allow it for practical reasons.

There were some points on which Mother and Father Van Exem disagreed. The healthy tensions that ensued between these two strong characters, each wanting to have his or her own way, resulted in a remarkable equilibrium.

The first draft of the Constitutions, drawn up by Mother Teresa, was given to Father de Gheldere for eventual correction. He improved the wording here and there, but otherwise made no changes. 'The Finger of God is here' he said, and respected the work he considered to be inspired by the Holy Spirit.

Christ, who lived in her, must have inspired, guided and sustained Mother as she wrote the Constitutions of the Institute that was to work entirely for His glory.

The Constitutions were the work of a woman who knows by personal experience 'the length and breadth, the height and depth of the love of Christ.' That love excels all human understanding, proceeding as it does from the Saviour's heart; that love the Spirit of Jesus pours into the hearts of those who eagerly open themselves to receive it.

Mother begins by stating the goal of those who will join the Institute, as revealed on the day of her inspiration:

'Our aim is to quench the infinite thirst of Jesus Christ for love by the profession of the evangelical counsels and by wholehearted free service to the poorest of the poor, according to the teaching and life of Our Lord in the Gospel, revealing in a unique way the Kingdom of God.

'Our particular mission is to labour at the salvation and sanctification of the poorest of the poor.

'As Jesus Christ was sent by His Father so He sends us too, filled with His Spirit to preach His Gospel of love and compassion to the poorest of the poor all over the world.

'It shall be our utmost endeavour to proclaim Jesus Christ to men of all nations, especially to those who are under our care.'

Then Mother states the fundamental duty of the Sisters, which flows from God's nature, His purpose in creating, the reason for His calling the Sisters to the religious life as expressed in the very name of the Congregation:

'We are called the MISSIONARIES OF CHARITY.

' "God is love." A Missionary of Charity must be a missionary of love. She must be full of charity in her own soul and spread that same charity to the souls of others, Christians and non-Christians.'

Mother's vision encircles the world in a passionate desire to make it answer the love of God and of Jesus Christ. It recalls to mind the great Rules of Benedict, Bernard, Francis, Ignatius.

The Constitutions charm by the kindness and gentleness, the balance and moderation they display, which do not weaken their passionate outburst of love for God and for his children. Tact and sensitiveness are apparent: the author is a woman.

In October 1950, on the Feast of the Most Holy Rosary, Mother received from Rome permission to start a new Congregation of Sisters destined to work among the poorest of the poor. Archbishop Périer came to celebrate Mass in their little chapel. Father Van Exem, who assisted him, read the bull received from Rome, sanctioning the existence of the Congregation of the Missionaries of Charity, approving and confirming the aim for which they were established. This gave great happiness to Mother and her young team of generous apostles. They sang the praises of the Lord in thanksgiving for his kind protection.

From this moment onwards the recruitment to the Congregation never slowed down. Candidates came in increasing numbers, from Bengal and Chota Nagpur, from the East Coast and South India, and also from foreign countries.

Sister Eugene speaks

The first candidate from Kerala to join the Missionaries of Charity came by way of Shillong, a hill station in the North-East. In
June 1976 I met her at Darjeeling; she was the Superior of the
house there; and asked her to tell me her recollections of the early
days.

'Tell me, Sister, what struck you most when you were in the
Upper Room right at the beginning?'

'I was number twenty-one. We all received a number in the
order in which we joined. I was only fifteen years old, still at
school at Shillong. I had come to work with the Sisters during
the holidays. But I got to like the work and stayed. At first I had
no idea of what the religious life meant; I was serving the poor
and found it stimulating. Only when I took my profession did I
really realize what it meant to be a religious.

'What struck me most was the spirit of faith, the tremendous
faith shown by Mother; we lived in that atmosphere. We
depended fully on God for everything. I remember two instances
when essential things were missing in the community. There was
no food for the evening meal; but Mother said 'Do not worry, it
will come.' And by the evening, someone, unexpectedly,
brought what was required.

'During the day I went to work in the dispensaries or the slum
schools.

'How many were you when you left Creek Lane?'

'Twenty-six.'

'And with Mother that would mean twenty-seven. Were you
not twenty-eight?'

'Perhaps. But before we left, we started praying very intently
to obtain the Home of Kalighat and a new house for the
novitiate. During about three months, we went in the evenings
in procession to Fatima Chapel. Father Henry had erected an
open chapel.'

'Yes, about two kilometres from St Teresa's Church, where
the church dedicated to Our Lady of Fatima stands now.'

'Well, Father Henry organized a procession every evening. He
accompanied the Sisters as we went through the Calcutta streets
saying the rosary aloud. Some lay people came to join us. And
from six to about nine, we went on the road from our house to
the Church of St Teresa's and thence to Fatima chapel, praying

there and again on our way home. We were asking Our Lady of Fatima to obtain for us the new house we needed to expand our novitiate, and also the refuge for the dying of Kalighat.

'After a full day of work we were on our feet walking and praying. We truly stormed Heaven to obtain these two houses. We forgot that we were tired, so caught were we by enthusiasm for our work. God had to give it; Our Lady was to help us obtain it. And God granted our prayer. Kalighat was turned over to us. Immediately we went to work there. As I was not yet a novice, I went every day.'

'Did Mother go with you daily?'

'Yes, she came with us and worked with us; but not daily. The Sisters took turns; sometimes Sister Dorothy, sometimes Sister Gertrude and some others. We received much help from Mrs Chater, a Chinese lady.'

'Yes, I knew her well. She was devoted, generous, and a good organizer. Business-like, efficient, she would certainly fit in with Mother's style of work.'

'She took us in her car daily, at the beginning, when we did not know Calcutta well and the trams and buses we would have had to take to reach Kalighat, which was very far from our house. Mrs Chater took us at eight in the morning and brought us back at three in the afternoon. We ate something there. I fed the patients, sponged them, and so on. Mrs Chater often sent the food for the inmates. Then her cook came and prepared things on the premises. He was a Moslem; he became so attached to the place that he stayed at night, and after some time worked only there. He died still in harness. He had a deep devotion to Our Lady and decorated her altar for her feast days.'

'Did you experience any opposition?'

'From where?'

'From people of the locality or other groups?'

I was told by Mother that there had been difficulties at the beginning.

'Mother did not tell us anything. We did our work and then returned to Creek Lane. We continued going there from the new house. We shifted to the new novitiate only after some time. I remained there and became a novice. Kalighat became our first big work.'

'It was something quite distinctive. Before that you only had dispensaries and small schools as other religious institutes also have.'

'Yes, Kalighat was the result of Mother's faith and the prayers of all.'

'Truly it was Our Lady's gift to the Missionaries of Charity, that you might devote yourselves there to the glory of Jesus, her Son.'

The second floor at 14 Creek Lane was now full. Mother had taken every available room, and also the annexe. Applications from candidates came in increasing numbers. The works were developing and becoming more diversified. The Holy Spirit indicated that it was time to give up the friendliness and intimacy of the Upper Room, to 'launch into the deep', and to prepare to spread out the apostolic endeavours of the Sisters throughout the world.

Mother Teresa could repeat after St Paul, with full strength, and the Senior Sisters could gently echo her words: 'I have been through my initiation, and now I am ready for anything, anywhere. There is nothing I cannot master with the help of the One who gives me strength.' (*Phil. 4, 12–13*)

4. Pentecost

'When Pentecost day came around they heard what sounded like a powerful wind from heaven, the noise of which filled the entire house. . . . They were all filled with the Holy Spirit and began to speak foreign languages as the Spirit gave them the gift of speech.'

(*Acts 2, 1–4*)

In February 1953 Mother Teresa, her novices and postulants moved to larger premises, to what is still the Mother-house of the Congregation. Mother brought with her the picture of the Immaculate Heart of Mary which had stood above the altar in their chapel.

The spirit of Pentecost soon invaded the new house. Like the apostles, the Sisters were united in prayer around Mary the Mother of Jesus. Full of confidence, they rejoiced because the Lord is risen, has appeared to Peter and has shown himself alive to his disciples. Gloriously risen he now manifests his power to us.

God our Father who accepted the sacrifice of Christ, and raised him from the dead, had also rewarded the sacrifice of Mother Teresa and her Sisters. Their Institute and Constitutions had been approved by the Authorities of the Church. In April 1953, at the Cathedral of the Most Holy Rosary, the first group of Sisters took their first vows and Mother Teresa her final vows in the Congregation.

Now the Sisters had a house of their own to receive and train postulants and novices. The new house, at 54A Lower Circular Road stood some ten minutes from the parish church of St Teresa where Mother had opened a dispensary, and twenty minutes from the 'Cenacle' in the house of the Gomes family.

The Sisters were able to occupy a three-storeyed house which was part of a small complex of buildings erected around a courtyard. The Sisters erected a statue of Our Lady in a conspicuous place. Since Mother did not have the money to buy the property, Archbishop Périer advanced her the sum. By shouldering the risk he proved his sympathy and effective support for the Missionaries of Charity. The age of large generous donations had not yet arrived. The Sisters lived in the years of pure faith and uncertainty of the morrow, but Mother says that the thought of having to repay debts contracted in the name of Almighty God never troubled her. It was for His glory and the service of His children.

When the house was bought for her, Mother objected: 'What shall we do with such a large house?' But the Lord God soon sent her postulants and novices to fill it.

Vocations came in increasing numbers. It was as at the beginning of the Church when the disciples rejoiced, seeing God's power call more and more members to be added to the glory of the Lord.

With more members they could expand and diversify their works of charity: visits to the slums, slum schools, dispensaries, home for the dying, soon a home for abandoned and crippled children, work among tuberculosis patients, work among leprosy patients, training for poor girls, adoption plans for orphaned children.

God's visible protection and the infusion of his Spirit filled them with optimism; they were a dynamic group, contagiously enthusiastic.

As at Pentecost, the Holy Spirit gave them a character of *universality*, as participates in the universal mission of the Church. Sisters from different parts of India, speaking various languages, came to join their ranks.

Support came from all sides: from the Archbishop of Calcutta and many priests; from the Chief Minister of West Bengal, and later from the Prime Minister of India; from scores of Indian friends – Christian and non-Christian – from groups of American and British ladies.

Charitable Agencies sent supplies of foodstuffs and medicines; the local and national press praised the work, whilst international reviews also became interested in the young Congregation.

Like the apostles, the Sisters are witnesses to Christ's death and resurrection and to His glorious exaltation in heaven; their lives, their works proclaim Him as the Lord, who, after redeeming mankind on the cross and rising up to a glorious life, has sent the Holy Spirit upon them. Through His power they perform their service to God and men. (*Acts 2, 22 ff*) The Sisters could also say:

'All of us are witnesses that God raised Jesus to life ... what you see and hear is the outpouring of that Spirit.'

They are witnesses to the nations. Many see it, and, perturbed by this fact, ask us: 'How can they go on with this life among the down-trodden?' The answer is:

'They do it by the power of Jesus.'

Like the first disciples of Jesus, the Sisters 'remained faithful to the teaching of the apostles, to the brotherhood, to the breaking of bread and to the prayers. They all lived together and owned everything in common. They shared their food gladly and generously; they praised God and were looked up to by everyone.' (*Acts, 2, 42–47*)

This 'brotherhood' or 'fellowship' implies a united purpose and also concern for the poorer members, so that everything is pooled in common; which shows perfect charity.

Thus, the young Missionaries of Charity relived the first years of the Christian Church, by their faith, by their optimism, their joy, strong in their belief that they belong to Jesus who sends them to bring to all men the Good News of God's love and redemption.

The Holy Spirit filled them with charity, an active charity manifesting itself in an unquenchable desire to help their neighbours to God.

The group was animated by a healthy enthusiasm, resulting from the belief that theirs was God's work and from the certainty that the Lord Himself had inspired and still animated their young Congregation. His protection was evident as they went forth, progressing in numbers.

We see among them the same happiness at the growth of their community that had possessed the members of the early Church: 'day by day the Lord added to their community'. It was his call; he supplied the grace. Mother repeated to them the words of Christ: 'I chose you, you did not choose Me.' It kept the young novices and soon the young professed in humility: the merit was not theirs, the call came from God. It gave them great confidence, for the Lord who calls also gives the grace necessary to obey His call.

Joy was manifested by their singing of hymns and canticles; by their prayer in common and in private. By their dedication they made of themselves daily to the Lord as they repeated together: 'Lord make me an instrument of your peace. . . .'

Yes, an instrument: I wish to be supple, obedient, docile in Your Hand. Mother put before them the three virtues she wished would characterize them: total surrender — trust — cheerfulness.

There were other similarities between the young Church and the young Institute which was now part of the great Catholic Church.

At the beginning of the Church, a man called Simon Magus was struck by the power the Apostles had of giving the Holy Spirit to the believers and by the extraordinary works they did; he asked them to give them that power, even for a consideration, which of course the Apostles did not do. Peter rebuked him, saying 'May your silver be lost for ever, and you with it, for thinking that money could buy what God gave for nothing.' In a similar way, the influence the Sisters acquired over people through the good works they performed by the grace of the Holy Spirit, and their example of brotherly love moved some Communist workers to approach them and ask them to share with them the secret of their attraction and power.

Mother told me: 'Communist workers in Calcutta, especially in the Entally area, want to know the secret of the Sisters' influence. Why do poor people listen to the Sisters and not to the Communists who promise them comfort on earth. There is no secret; the Sisters preach and practise love.'

Some time later Mother told me: 'I met in Delhi an official of the Ministry of Relief and Rehabilitation who is very much impressed by our work. He gives us all the help he can. Now he has written to me, asking if I could train some of his officers. He would send a batch of some twenty to be trained by us for three months and would pay all their expenses. He hopes that thus they would imbibe our spirit and follow our methods. Do you think I should accept? And would you give them lectures if they came here? I cannot do the whole work myself.'

We discussed the matter. The gentleman seemed to be mistaken about the reason for the Sisters' success and influence on the people. He thought they had evolved some new technique and used some method not described in the textbooks of sociology. How could their approach to the people be assimilated and emulated? Other official agencies had also asked her how she succeeded in getting the confidence of the poor; why did people trust her; and what made her Sisters devote themselves to such an extent?

'Mother, I would suggest that you inform this gentleman that what activates your Sisters is their motivation, which cannot be passed on to professional people who do not believe in Christ. We can at most deal with ten persons at a time. Send them by batches of two to accompany your Sisters every morning, see how they work, and give them one or two talks in the evening. But they will not relish this programme. They cannot imitate your Sisters.'

I tried to draft a programme, and devise a system of motivation that might agree with the beliefs and feelings of the officials. Of course, if they had the spirit of devotedness, if they believed in a humanitarian cause, we could help them in some way. But without a firm belief in God and in man as God's child, in the dignity of every man, the poor, the lepers, the slow-witted, the abandoned, how could they enter into our spirit?

A week later we discussed the matter again. Mother informed the Officer in Delhi of the difficulties of the project and what we were prepared to do. Nothing came out of the proposal, as we had expected.

A cause of deep frustration and disappointment was the provision of Canon Law forbidding new Institutes to open houses outside the diocese during ten years after their inception. On that point the Archbishop was adamant: 'Mother, you may not start any house outside the diocese before ten years are completed.'

Mother felt an irresistible urge to go forward to spread, develop, occupy new territory, start new houses, new ventures. Her active temperament was coupled with an unquenched zeal. Needs were great, whilst time was short; why these delays?

This meant that between forty and fifty years of age, when a person's activity is normally at its peak, while she was burning with the desire to produce, to start new ventures, during those strong creative years, she was to sit still and wait.

She was told to concentrate on training her personnel, especially future superiors. She was to learn later the wisdom of the Church's law; ten years to build up a team and fill it with a new spirit, pattern it on the simplicity of the Gospel, and to mould women of character, capable of taking charge of new foundations, was not excessive.

Once Mother saw a chance of opening a house outside the diocese of Calcutta. The offer, the call even, came from Father Harrison, who had sent her many candidates from Chota Nagpur. As the parish priest of Mahuadan he had a house ready for Mother Teresa at Daltonganj in his parish, with a garden, a well, and all that the Sisters might need. He invited her to come and work there.

Mother asked Archbishop Périer for permission to accept this offer, but he could not grant this. Father Harrison was disappointed, but both from Mahuadan and from Noatoli, where he was moved, he sent girls to join the Missionaries of Charity in Calcutta; at times he sent as many as ten in one batch. He thus helped to give to the new Institute an all-India dimension and the possibility of opening houses in Hindi speaking areas.

The day the ten years probation period ended, Mother started houses in the archdioceses of Ranchi and Delhi and the diocese of Jhansi. Nothing would stop her now. Her pent-up energy and zeal poured themselves out with the full power the Spirit gave her.

In all fairness to the delay caused by the Church's prescription it should be said that when in 1976 she was asked:

'Mother, what is your greatest difficulty?' She answered:

'Superiors, Father. To find suitable superiors and keep them zealous when they are in charge. Once they exercise authority, they may lose the sense of poverty and do things independently.' In fact, several of the perpetual professed who left were or had been superiors.

The Novitiate

When I was appointed confessor and spiritual director of the novices and the postulants, Mother asked me: 'Please, Father, do not interfere in the running of the house. You know, some

Fathers want me to change certain things. For instance, they tell me that the Sisters should have fans in the common room or in the chapel. I do not want them to have fans. The poor whom they are to serve have no fans. Most of the girls come from village homes where they had no fans. They should not be more comfortable here than at home. The same for the routine of the house. Please do not interfere.'

I told her 'Mother, I shall not interfere in material things; I have been appointed spiritual adviser; that is my province; I shall not go beyond that.' She trusted me, since she had asked the Archbishop to appoint me. We always had the best of relations. I respected her judgement, admired her zeal and spirit of faith, envied her humility and charity.

Mother had much experience of the spiritual life, its problems and requirements. She gave stimulating spiritual conferences to her Sisters, speaking four or even five times a day, to different groups.

The novices were 'hand tooled' receiving personal attention from Mother. When the number of new foundations started growing she had to leave the Mother-house more often, and the burden of forming the novices fell on the shoulders of Sister Agnes, the Mistress of novices, of Sister Frederick, her assistant, and of other Sisters, later put in charge of groups of novices.

When I started, there were about thirty-five novices and postulants. After a year or two there were fifty, later sixty-five, then eighty-five, then the number reached one hundred. It was wonderful to see how the Lord blessed the young Institute. Candidates arrived from various parts of India and also from abroad. Twice a year some novices took their vows; they were soon replaced by others. Larger numbers meant more work for the confessor. My weekly task started with a spiritual instruction; then there was a holy hour during which I began hearing confessions and the exercise went on, from three o'clock till five, six and seven p.m., as the number of novices increased. It even became necessary to devote two afternoons to them to have more time for the spiritual direction of the Sisters.

For some months the novitiate was shifted to a house on Park Street. But later the novices returned to the Mother-house and junior Sisters were lodged in the house in Park Street.

For many years I went every week to the Mother-house. No one ever brought me tea or anything else; there was a glass of water in the sacristy. I felt that was normal; since the Sisters did not take any refreshments, why should their confessor have a more comfortable life than theirs? The material side of life, creature comforts, seemed to count for nothing. I had been allowed to join an expedition, difficult and thrilling; hardships were part of the game, real practical poverty had to be experienced. I felt indeed grateful that the Sisters accepted me, who came from a more comfortable house, as a part of the team, and let me live their life for a while.

Now things have changed. The heroic days are over. More consideration is shown for the poor human body, aging and suffering. After a talk, the Sisters may request you to stay for a while and take some refreshments.

When of late, Mother saw me removing my shoes and walking on the cold cement floor, she came to me and insisted:

'Father, please keep your shoes on, otherwise you will catch cold.'

'But Mother, you walk barefooted, can I not do it also?'

'We are accustomed, Father, and you are not.'

This was like Paul writing to Timothy, the old fighter showing his concern for a fellow worker: 'Timothy, take a glass of wine; it will help your weak stomach.' To crown heroic detachment and the mortification of all human affections and desires, there is kindness and gentleness.

The novices were very similar to the novices of other religious congregations. They exhibited the same desire for holiness, generosity in making sacrifices, eagerness to progress on the way to perfection. They belonged to the same race as their sisters, friends and neighbours who joined other Institutes, without knowing them very well.

But one sensed — or was it only imagination — a definite spiritual quality, that particular brand of enthusiasm, joy and submission to the guidance of the Holy Spirit, which are found specially in all new religious ventures relying on deep faith and trust in God.

The community lived in circumstances that brought it close to the original Pentecost. They could see God's hand in their foundation. They needed more faith in God's day to day protection than the well established Institutes; they needed more simplicity, the 'one step enough for me' process and progress, which brought its own reward: simplicity, trust, joy.

The few novices or Sisters with intellectual problems or complicated minds, those worried by the inadequacy of present political and social structures, did not persevere very long in the Institute. Partly on this account, and partly for reasons of the material conditions of life, the few foreign candidates and novices presented their confessor with as many problems as the Indian Sisters who were ten or fifteen times as numerous.

Obviously for a novice from Germany, the U.K. or Malta, climate and living conditions at the Mother-house were a challenge requiring an unusual dose of courage and self-denial. And so some went home. A fair number remained, went through the training and became excellent professed nuns. Indian novices hailing from comfortable homes and arriving with a university degree found the way of life no less uncomfortable, but could better foresee what their life would be than those who came to India for the first time.

I did my best to foster in the generous young recruits to the religious life, love for God and total surrender to his guidance, in a joyful offering of their service. Mother often came to listen to the instructions, sitting on the floor like the novices. When it was time for the sacrament of penance, she took her place among the Sisters.

Often Mother would come to the parlour, when confessions and adoration were over, to talk of spiritual matters and apprise me of the progress of the Institute and its works. The praise of God was always on her lips; she never complained of any hardship. We never disagreed or had any argument. She wanted a serious, solid spiritual formation to be given to her Sisters, and it was her responsibility to see that they received it.

It was good at times to hear a senior Sister remark: 'Mother doesn't see; she can't understand. . . .' They were fully obedient to their Superior, but showed mature judgement and ability to think for themselves, as also interest in the well-being and progress of the Congregation. These Sisters had to prepare themselves to shoulder responsibilities and take decisions – even if at times they would be blamed for them. A Superior must be able to decide for herself, after due consultation, and cannot be expected to be always right.

They had special problems. Food was one of them, but not in the manner we would have expected.

'At the Holy Family Hospital at Patna,' said Mother, 'the Superior told me: "You must feed your Sisters well. They will have much work, and move among the sick in unhealthy localities; to resist disease they must be well fed."'

'And so the penance of the Sisters is to eat what they are given; they should not deprive themselves of what they need to be good workers. Their penance is not to choose, but to eat their portion and obey.'

This posed a problem for the spiritual director. Several times young novices asked 'What must I do? I cannot eat what is put on my plate. I have made frantic efforts to eat it and swallow it. They give me four chappattis, which is too much for me. What should I do?'

The rule was for their good; they required strong nourishment, being out much of the day, visiting homes, nursing the sick, often performing hard work.

Once the Sisters discussed together the matter of food. So many people are going hungry; should the Sisters not reduce their own consumption? They might perhaps do with only three chappattis per head for one of their meals? The question was considered by those in charge. Mother argued from the standpoint of her Sisters' health. Some nuns in other congregations and also in her own suffered from tuberculosis. She did not want this to happen to her Sisters if it could be prevented.

A few days later, one of the Sisters announced smilingly: 'The question of the chappattis has been decided. Instead of four, we are to get five per head and eat them with obedience.'

From the start, Mother Teresa received much encouragement from Dr B. C. Roy, the eminent statesman who for many years presided over the fortunes of West Bengal as its Chief Minister. A giant of a man, in more senses than one, who seldom appeared at public functions or political rallies, he administered what Nehru once called 'the problem State' with remarkable ability, competence and assiduity.

To meet him, Mother, at the beginning of her career, went at six o'clock in the morning to the free medical consultation he gave every day for an hour at his residence. A medical practitioner of repute who attended on celebrities like Gandhi, Nehru and the King of Nepal, he kept in touch with the medical art by giving daily free consultations to those who approached him. A few persons seized this occasion to present him with their petitions.

The scene was worth seeing. Admitted by his secretary, the patients sit on benches or chairs along the walls of the hall near the entrance. Doctor Roy goes round, looks at a patient's face, his eyes, his tongue, puts his stethoscope to his chest, feels his stomach and asks a few questions. He quickly sizes up the situation, and has an extraordinary gift of diagnosis; prescribes, advises, passes on to the next patient. The whole thing is done in public, without wasting a moment. All feel members of a great family and trust the famous doctor.

Mother does not come to consult him about her health but to put forward the case of some poor people who need help or redress. Could she obtain a water connection for a slum? Electric light for another? The Chief Minister signs a memo addressed to the Officer-in-charge. It is as good as an order. 'Please enquire into the matter.' – 'Please look into this complaint.' After a few such requests, he has noticed the little nun who cares only for others; and they are not people of influence, but always poor.

Soon Doctor Roy tells Mother to call on him at his office. Later he will tell her that she need not make an appointment but just come in whilst he is at his desk, where he works most of the day. Thus began a real partnership, with the two of them trusting one another, working together for the good of the poor. He a man of immense experience, wielding powers in the whole State; she a fledgling in the work of uplift and organization, but strong with the power of her divine Lord. Doctor Roy was a member of the Brahmo Samaj, a believer in one God, excluding all image worship, deeply respecting Jesus Christ and his teachings.

Soon it was he who urged Mother on.

'Dr Roy wants me to expand Sishu Bhavan,' Mother told me. He said 'Bigger, Mother, bigger. We have so much misery here. Our problems are enormous.'

Another time, she said: 'Dr Roy asked me if we could take charge of the government-run Vagrancy Homes in Calcutta.'

'How many are there?' I asked.

'Four. He told me "I trust you. I shall not ask you for any accounts. You will have no financial problem. Just put your nuns in charge of these houses." But I had to refuse. I do not have enough Sisters. I do not want to put too many of them into the same work. There is too much to be done.'

It was true at the time. But also I suspect that she did not want to take over other people's work. In this case she would certainly have made enemies among the officials, which she always tried to avoid. 'Dr Roy never gave me money,' said Mother, 'but his protection, his recommendation to an official department was worth much more than money.'

At times they differed, even strongly disagreed. Both of them had too much character to bow down easily. Mother argued for the Leper Asylum Dr Roy wanted to remove from Calcutta's neighbourhood, since the town was expanding. I think he was right. He saw the good of the local population; Mother fought for the lepers who were finally moved to some other place. At least she got them a decent home.

Doctor Roy paid Mother this greatest tribute on his eightieth birthday. On that memorable anniversary, he went to work as usual at his office. Reporters called on him and enquired 'How do you feel on your eightieth birthday, still being Chief Minister?' He did not answer 'I thought of Mahatma Gandhi, with whom I fought for Independence, or of Jawaharlal Nehru, my friend and India's Prime Minister,' or make any other personal recollection. He said simply; 'As I climbed the steps leading to my office, I thought of Mother Teresa who devotes her life to the welfare of the poor'. The next day it was front-page news in the papers. No one could any longer ignore the humble nun in a blue-bordered white saree, who saw Christ in the poorest of the poor.

5. Service of Love

'I was hungry and you gave me food; I was thirsty and you gave me drink; I was naked and you clothed me; I was sick or in prison and you visited me. Whenever you did this to the least of my brothers you did it to me.'

(*Matt. 25, 35–40*)

'In the choice of the works of the apostolate,' said Mother, 'there was neither planning nor preconceived ideas. We started work as needs and opportunities arose. God showed what he wanted us to do.'

So they began schools for the poorest children of the slums, dispensaries, Sunday schools to teach the children prayer, craft schools that the poor might learn how to earn a living.

The first big work of the Missionaries of Charity was the Kalighat Home for the Dying, begun whilst they still lived at 14 Creek Lane. Michael Gomes remembers vividly how the search for a place to house the dying destitute started.

'One day, we saw alongside the Campbell Hospital (now the Nilratan Sarkar Hospital) close to our house, a man dying on the roadside. Mother enquired; the hospital authorities could not accommodate him. We went to a chemist to get some medicine for him; when we returned with the medicines, the man was dead on the street. Mother did not hide her feelings. "They look after a dog or a cat better than a fellow-man," she said. They would not allow that to happen to their pets.' She went to the Commissioner of Police to complain about this state of affairs. That was the origin of the Kalighat Home for the Dying.

'Are you positive on this point? The story as written by journalists is usually that Mother saw a woman on a pavement, full of sores, with maggots in her wounds. She stayed with her the whole night, keeping the rats away from her, and in the morning the woman died in her arms.'

'That is not the truth. First, Mother never stayed out at night whilst she was in our house, not a single night. And Kalighat Home was started from our house. I was with her when the man died on the street, in front of the hospital where he had not been admitted.'

Such occurrences were not exceptional; Mother must have seen more than once destitute persons lying on the pavements, sick or at death's door. She herself narrated that one day she came across a dying woman on a pavement close to a hospital, who had festering wounds and was lying on a piece of sackcloth. Mother succeeded in getting the woman admitted into a hospital. Something had to be done about it; she moved heaven and earth to this end. It is no exaggeration to say that she moved heaven since the young Missionaries of Charity went for several weeks to pray to the Shrine of our Lady of Fatima. That she moved earth at the same time is evident: she approached the Commissioner of Police who was most happy to help her to find a place and remove this blot on Calcutta's reputation. Mother also approached Dr Ahmed, the Health Officer of the Corporation, for a place to receive the more hopeless cases, the persons dying on the street; 'Give me at least a room' she pleaded.

Calcutta has excellent doctors and very good hospitals and nursing homes. There are free beds in the hospitals. But the city's population was swollen by an influx of refugees at the time of partition, and of villagers in periods of scarcity. Thus the number of beds to receive the huge number of sick people proves insufficient. Naturally the hospitals prefer to admit patients who have a hope of recovery rather than those dying of old age or malnutrition.

Mother Teresa offered to take care of the homeless destitute, sick, starving, those dying on the streets. She needed a house, but had neither the funds nor credit. An empty wing in a rest house for pilgrims was found; it was attached to the famous temple of the Goddess Kali in South Calcutta. Mother Teresa was allowed to use the building 'provisionally'. From this day one of the headaches of the Police Commissioner was removed. The city's social-minded citizens felt relieved. No one could write any more to newspapers lamenting the state of affairs in a city in which some people were allowed to die without a roof, without food, without medical care.

The help of the police proved useful in another way. Mother knew that to open a house where food and shelter can be had for the asking in Calcutta is to invite an endless rush of candidates. Hence it was decided that only persons brought by the police would be admitted.

The home, or hospital, Mother called Nirmal Hriday: the Immaculate Heart of Mary. It can accommodate about sixty men and sixty women inmates in two wards. Over thirty thousand destitute have been admitted. Half of them died in the home, decently, peacefully, prayerfully. The Sisters and their co-workers washed them, fed them, consoled them, cheered their spirits, prepared their souls so that, rejoicing in the hope of a happy life in heaven, each one of them might 'die with God'.

Some opposition was to be expected. The Home stood on sacred temple ground. The Kalighat temple, which enjoys tremendous popularity and a considerable income, is served by four hundred priests. Recalling the first days of that new venture, Michael Gomes says: 'At first there was opposition. A group of young people said that Mother was coming to convert people to Christianity here in the centre of Hinduism.

'A political leader told the young men that he would get her out. He came to see the place. Mother offered to take him round. He answered he could see things by himself and needed nobody to take him round. As he went round, he saw the miserable emaciated bodies, the sunken eyes, the Sisters washing the sores, feeding the hungry, distributing medicines, giving injections, all in a gentle, loving manner.

'When he came out he met some of the young men. He told them: "I promised I would get that woman out of here, and I shall. But, listen to me, I shall not get her out of this place before you get your mothers and sisters to do the work these nuns are doing. In the temple you have a Goddess in stone; here you have a living Goddess." That was the end of the opposition organized by this group.

'The Sisters went on caring for sick bodies and drooping spirits with a holy unconcern for outside murmurs. They had God's approval, that was enough for them, But their charity could not fail to impress many visitors. It happened one day that a priest of the temple, who suffered from tuberculosis, sought and found a welcoming haven in the Sisters' hospital. The service rendered to one of theirs made a deep impression on several of his brethren.'

Mother told me at the time:

'One morning, as I was washing the patients, a priest of the temple entered the ward. He prostrated himself before me, touched my feet with his hands which he then laid on his head. Then he stood up and said "For thirty years I have served the Goddess Kali in her temple. Now, the Goddess Mother stands before me in human form. It is my privilege today to worship the Mother present to my eyes." '

Later, Mother said:

'The question of the Kalighat Home for the Dying is to come up at a Corporation meeting. Some people object to destitute persons being brought there to die, on religious grounds; they say it defiles the place.'

'Mother, you know how these things are decided. It will be one item on a crowded agenda. The chairman will announce; Item No. 67, Mother Teresa runs a Home for the Dying in a building belonging to the Kalighat temple. Are there any objections? Should she be allowed to continue or asked to vacate the place? So, Mother, you need an influential Councillor to fight your battle and another one to support him. Then you will be allowed to remain until a more suitable place can be found – which means that you stay for good.'

And so it was. Some days later Mother was happy to report:

'At the Corporation meeting only two members objected on religious grounds. Nobody offered to provide a better place. So the resolution was passed that we are allowed to remain at Kalighat until a suitable place is found to accommodate the dying. My friends told me: "Do not worry. The objection has been duly registered and put into cold storage." '

The Calcutta Corporation supported the Kalighat Home for the Dying with a monthly subsidy. One day Mother informed the Corporation that she was no more in need of their help, and the subsidy was stopped.

A new house, Prem Dan, was given to the Missionaries of Charity by I.C.I. in 1975. After the inauguration ceremony, I asked Mother: 'Will you shift Nirmal Hriday of Kalighat to Prem Dan? She replied: 'I shall never give up Kalighat, unless they eject me forcibly.' Soon she had filled the new house with needy persons. In Calcutta there was no difficulty in doing this. As for Kalighat's Nirmal Hriday, the Home for the Dying has become a hallowed place. Its very ground has been made holy by the countless acts of love, of devotion, of those who nurse the sick with limitless patience; a place sanctified by the total surrender to God of so many who from there left earth for heaven – a sacred place which all believers enter as respectfully and silently as they enter a temple – because as Mother put it tersely: 'God is here.'

Prem Dan is used as a home for those who have a better chance to recover and survive; they can be kept there longer if need be, until they are back on their feet. It serves also for other classes of needy persons. Kalighat remains as a home for the dying destitute who have little chance of surviving.

With the inception of the Kalighat Home for the Dying it was hoped that destitute persons would no longer die on the Calcutta pavements. Well, not quite. It was impossible to completely stop this scandal in a city officially numbering one hundred thousand pavement dwellers with no other abode, and unofficially a good few thousands more.

The children's homes

The care of orphans, of abandoned or crippled children, has always been a preferred work of religious institutes.

Most Catholic centres in India and other countries have one or more orphanages, and facilities to receive orphans in their boarding schools.

Jesus himself gave us the example of love for children, who are naturally trustful, simple, loving.

'Jesus then took a little child, set him in front of the Twelve, put His arms around him, and said to them, "Anyone who welcomes one of these children in My name, welcomes Me; and anyone who welcomes Me welcomes not Me but the one who sent Me." ' (*Mar 9, 36–37*)

Later, adds St Mark, 'people were bringing little children to Him, for Him to touch them. The disciples turned them away, but when Jesus saw this he was indignant and said to them, "Let the little children come to Me; do not stop them; for it is to such as these that the kingdom of God belongs. I tell you solemnly, anyone who does not welcome the kingdom of God like a child will never enter it." Then he put His arms around them, laid His hands on them and gave His blessings.' (*Mark 10, 13–16*)

So it is a duty and a source of joy to minister to the children Jesus loves, and to serve Our Lord in the person of the child.

'How did the first Children's Home start, Brother Michael?'

'Well,' he answered, 'Mother had been looking for some time for a house where she could receive and care for unwanted children. One day as she came home she told me: "Mrs X. asked me to pray for her husband that he may stop drinking. He drinks a full bottle of whisky every day, and the market price of imported whisky is ninety rupees per bottle. Well, if Mr X can pay ninety rupees per day for his drinks, I can pay five hundred rupees a month for that house on Lower Circular Road which is to let. I shall take it and start a children's home." '

I remarked to a Sister: 'I cannot see the logic of arguing from the cost of a bottle of whisky.'

'No,' she replied, 'you men go by logic. We women follow our intuition, and we are more often right than you.'

'Here, you are correct, Sister. Your intuition is based on love and it is more often right than our dry reasonings.'

This was another case requiring trust in God. Was the work really needed for His glory? If so, His Providence would see that the means did not fail. He would take care of the work started for Him.

And so the house was rented.

There were so many problems, so many needs: unwanted children, unwedded mothers who could not have their baby at home nor take him back there, orphans, crippled children, mentally retarded children to be looked after.

Catholic charity was already active in the field: the Franciscan Missionaries of Mary had a creche where the police would bring abandoned infants. There were other orphanages. But the needs of Calcutta seemed inexhaustible.

And so Sishu Bhavan, the Children's Home, was started.

Abandoned infants were brought by the police and by private parties. Some of them were found in dustbins – not many, let us be fair. Some were left at the doors of convents. Others were brought by people who did not want to reveal their names.

One infant was found lying before the altar of the Blessed Sacrament in my own Church of the Sacred Heart, by the sacristan when he opened the church doors in the morning. The child was crying. The sacristan fetched some milk, made the child drink it, and soon the baby fell asleep, happy. The police were informed, and the baby duly taken to Mother Teresa's Sishu Bhavan. He was adopted by a Catholic family and is doing well.

Some infants are sickly or crippled. Some die soon, but many recover, become strong and healthy.

In 1976 a picture of Mother Teresa fondling a smiling child appeared in Calcutta papers. She had just accepted to take charge of five babies abandoned by their mothers in the maternity ward of one of Calcutta's main hospitals. Later it was announced that the authorities of the hospital had another hundred and two babies or infants who had been similarly left behind by their mothers after their delivery. Mother Teresa declared that she would take charge of all the abandoned babies.

After showing such willingness to help the civil and medical authorities to solve their human problems, it is not astonishing that she obtained their full co-operation for schemes for the betterment of the lot of the poor. She assumes the duty of charity whether or not she has the means. God will provide, she says.

In most localities where the Missionaries of Charity are established they receive unwanted or crippled children.

Sishu Bhavan in Calcutta has been for many years the centre of varied activities. Apart from receiving abandoned children and cripples, it is a place where some unwedded mothers stay whilst expecting their child. There also are stored food supplies to be distributed free to the poor.

Walking past the house on an afternoon, you may see fifty or eighty women with small children, waiting for the distribution to start. No distribution means for some of them no food for that day.

There are hazards and dangers in the free distribution of food.

'Mother has been seen,' says Michael Gomes, 'pushing back with unexpected physical strength a whole line of women rushing forward to receive rations.'

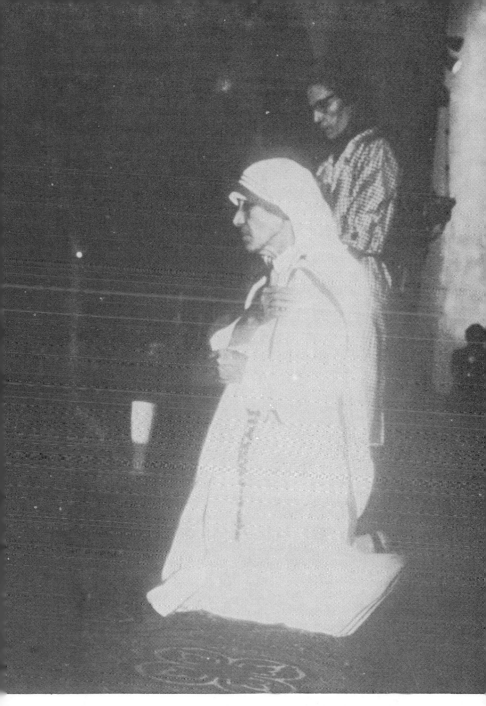

1. Mother Teresa in prayer. A church in Germany 1976.
In the background stands Miss Jacqueline de Decker.

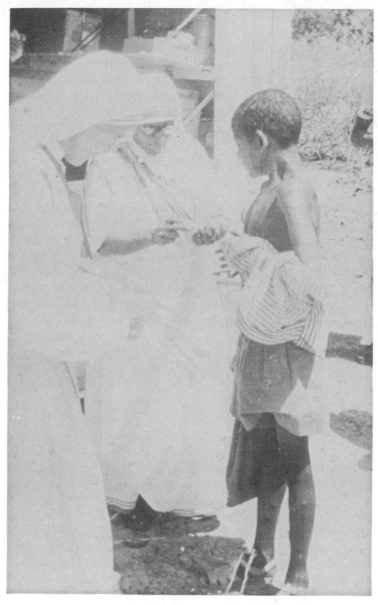

2. Treating a leper on the roadside from the back
of a mobile clinic.

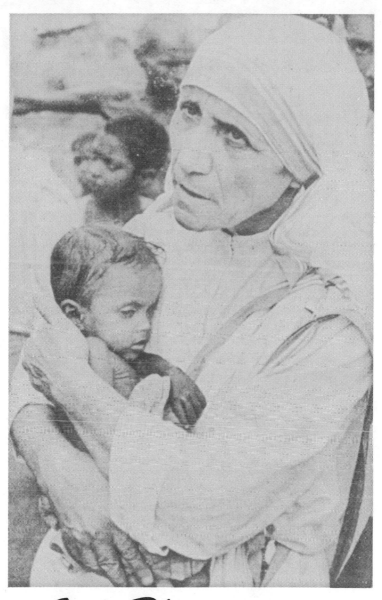

God Bless you

M. Teresa MC

4. Novices at prayer.

5. Professed sisters—brides of Christ.

The Sisters also have experienced some unpleasant moments when serving the poor. At Sishu Bhavan one day there was no stock to distribute rations to card-holders. The agency supplying the Sisters for this project had stopped sending foodstuffs to Calcutta to divert them to another area they considered more urgently in need. The Sisters were unable to give anything to the crowd standing at the gate. Some people manifested their anger by shouts and even tried to set fire to the house, whilst they abused the Sisters and accused them of robbing their food for their own benefit. But the police and the Fire Brigade appeared on the scene in a matter of minutes, thus saving the house, the children and the crippled living there.

The Sisters had other moments of danger. Close to Calcutta two Sisters were confronted by a group of lepers, displeased with the arrangements which had been made for them, who locked them inside their van, and started pushing it towards a canal. Fortunately another Sister called the police, who arrived in time to save the two Sisters from an enforced bath or worse. Such things are part of the work of charity.

The Sisters narrate their disagreeable adventures during the evening recreation.

Mother defends her policy.

'At a meeting in Bangalore', recalled Mother, 'a Sister attacked me for distributing food freely to the poor. She said that I spoiled the poor by my acts of charity. I answered her: "If I spoil the poor, you and the other Sisters spoil the rich in your select schools. And Almighty God is the first to spoil us. Does He not give freely to all of us? Then why should I not imitate my God and give freely to the poor what I have received freely" They had nothing to answer.'

Mother could have quoted St Paul's words to Timothy, 'God who, out of his riches, gives us all we need for our happiness.' (*Tim. 16, 17*)

Work among lepers

Mother Teresa was led to start working for the welfare of leprosy patients in an indirect way. It was again the force of circumstances, or to look at it with the eyes of faith, the Hand of God working through human instruments, that brought her into that particular field of charitable work.

For many years the Sisters of Charity had run a leper asylum at Gobra, on the outskirts of Calcutta. In this leper asylum lived one hundred and fifty inmates, well cared for by the Sisters. It happened that plans for the development of Calcutta covered the area of Gobra. The large compound including the houses occupied by the lepers was to be expropriated, to allow the locality to be developed in a planned manner. People would never accept housing close to an area they thought infected by germs of the dreaded disease. And so it was decided to take over the property occupied by the Sisters; the lepers would have to find some other shelter.

Mother Teresa, informed of the project, was indignant. What would happen to the poor sufferers? Where would they go? Who would provide them with a suitable place to live? Mother took up their cause and went to plead it before the Chief Minister. Dr Roy, her patron, listened to her; but he would not reverse the decision. Calcutta had to expand. The city was bursting at the seams; the housing problem defied solution. Suitable lodgings were to be provided for hundreds of thousands of people. A development project in an area contiguous to the city could not be stopped on account of a hundred and fifty lepers living in a colony with little contact with the outside world. They would be displaced.

At least Mother obtained that the lepers would not be removed before some alternative accommodation had been found for them.

The Chief Minister offered a place in Bankura District. Mother, not finding the place suitable, complained to him: 'You told me you would give the lepers a good place to live in, but the place you offer us lacks a good supply of water, which is essential for leprosy patients.'

Thus Mother became active in leper work. She started a Leprosy Collection Day. Collection tins were taken around Calcutta for Mother Teresa's Leprosy Fund, bearing the words: 'Touch the Leper with your kindness.' Money poured in from all sources.

'At the time of our Leprosy Day,' said the Sister in charge of finance, 'we just throw the cheques into a basket, so numerous are they.

'One can only admire Calcutta people, so anxious to help the lepers. Leper asylums and villages are needed in India, but they are not enough.'

'You missionaries do not seem to understand,' a high Government Official told me several years ago, 'that our problems are of a magnitude the developed countries do not suspect, certainly do not experience. Take the case of leprosy; in a leprosarium you can look after two or three hundred patients. But we have two million sufferers from leprosy in this country, out of the world figure of four million. So you do not offer any workable solution to the problem; you do not even scratch the surface. We need an approach to the masses, a method that will reach hundreds of thousands of people.'

He was right: and this could now be done. Dr Hemeryckx, a Belgian who had worked for several years in Central Africa, had come to India, and had introduced a method of treating lepers on a mass scale. He favoured leaving them at home, from where they could regularly attend mobile clinics. In this manner he reached a considerable number of sufferers; many who were ashamed of showing themselves would come to the clinic. Parents could remain with their children, at least when they were not dangerously contagious.

It may be mentioned that before leaving India Dr Hemeryckx was received by the then Prime Minister, Mr Nehru, who thanked him for his services and for showing the way to mass treatment of leprosy.

Mother Teresa went to see the centre established by Dr Hemeryckx, near Madras. Then she offered to collaborate with government agencies and doctors. And so the Sisters started medical assistance to the lepers in a big way. This work became one of their main activities in India.

There would still be a need for some institutions or villages where infectious cases, or lepers with no one to look after them, or unable to take care of themselves, could be received.

To this end Shanti Nagar, the 'Town of Peace', was founded as a colony and rehabilitation centre for lepers in the district of Burdwan.

The same grace that blessed Father Damian, a modern hero of

charity, may bless those who today devote their whole life to the apostolate among lepers.

Two or three Sisters at different times confided to me 'I think I have contracted the disease. What must I do?' They were still young and slightly afraid, though ready to accept; that may have been all God asked from them.

The doctors are rightly cautious, and give the Sisters and Brothers who work with them strict instructions.

'The doctor forbade me to touch some patients because they are actively contagious. What should I do?' a Sister asked.

'Obey the doctor, Sister. You should not run any unreasonable risk of contracting the disease. You must take all the precautions ordered by the doctor. Thus you will be able to serve the patients better and for a longer time.'

But these devoted brides of Christ know that if the Institute assumes this apostolate on a large scale, some Sisters may experience what it means to be attacked by leprosy. Thus a religious may be able to give witness to the lepers in a specially convincing manner, by carrying a leper's cross behind the Saviour. Nuns of other Congregations have suffered and are still suffering from the disease they caught whilst ministering to leprosy patients. And they bless the Lord for this grace.

Mother Teresa knows that the poor need belief in God more than other people. The poor need hope, they need God. Those who would deprive them of hope, their only solace, commit a crime against humanity. If these others wish to be self-sufficient, not to tend to an infinity of truth, goodness and beauty, let them be self-sufficient alone — but let them not rob others of their hope.

Mother and her Sisters bring the poor hope, eternal hope and belief in God's goodness. The Sisters, young and educated, bend over them, wash their sores, smile to them and cheer them whilst never uttering a rough word or losing their temper. Why do they treat unknown people as true brothers and sisters? And they do it, not for two or three years, but for a whole life time. Simple people are neither fools nor easily fooled; they are not blinded by sophiscation; their simple minds discover the truth; those women mirror God's love. Thus through their sufferings they come to God.

6. Witnesses of Christ to the Nations

'You will receive power when the Holy Spirit comes on you, and then
you will be my witnesses not only in Jerusalem, but throughout Judaea
and Samaria, and indeed to the ends of the earth.'

(*Acts 1, 8*)

Ten years had elapsed since the Congregation of the Missionaries
of Charity had been approved by Rome. The Sisters had been
trained. Together Mother and the Sisters had prayed, worked,
studied. The Spirit of God had lavished His gifts on them.

Conforming to their Lord Jesus Christ, they lived His life,
shared His passion for the salvation of men. They had heard from
Him secret words of friendship, they had learnt His intimate
thoughts and desires. Like the Apostles they had the promise of
Jesus, that he would send them the Holy Spirit, and His command to make Him known to the world.

'I shall send you the Spirit of truth; he will be my witness. And
you too will be witnesses, because you have been with me from
the beginning.' (*John 15, 26–27*)

The Sisters were ready to go out and bear witness to their
Lord. Calcutta was their Jerusalem, the starting point of their
apostolate, which had its roots there; but the tree was to spread its
branches and bear fruit in many parts of the world.

They had the same purpose as the Apostles: to bear witness to
the Father's love for men, who loved us so much that He sent His
only begotten Son; to Christ's love for us, who died for our sins,
that we might become the Father's children of adoption, in and
through Him; to the love of the Spirit who pours into our hearts
His choice gifts; love for God and for all men.

Their Constitutions told them to bring the Good News to the
poor, to the poorest of the poor. This had been given as a sign of
the coming of the Saviour; a sign that the Kingdom of God had

appeared among the people: 'the Good News is preached to the poor.'

The third phase of the life of the young Congregation was beginning. Mother did not waste a single day. Some bishops, aware of the Sisters' work in Calcutta, wished to obtain their services; they requested Mother Teresa to establish houses in their dioceses.

India

The Sisters went first to Ranchi, then to Delhi, then to Jhansi. The Ranchi or Chota Nagpur Mission had previously belonged to the Calcutta Archdiocese. The Church now fully established in the region was the most lively young church in North India. From Ranchi Archdiocese many candidates had joined the Missionaries of Charity. It was only fair that the archdiocese should be rewarded for its generous gift of personnel. At the Archbishop's invitation Mother opened a house in Ranchi.

Next came Delhi. Archbishop Joseph Fernandes had known Mother Teresa during his many years in Calcutta as Vicar General and Auxiliary Bishop. Archbishop Knox, the Pro-Nuncio, was also interested in Mother Teresa's work. Since the number of local Catholics in Delhi was small, to strengthen the Catholic presence in the capital, the policy was to bring religious congregations from other parts of the country, to open schools and institutions that would benefit the people.

Mother found it useful to be close to the centre of government, to the ministries, to the offices of agencies providing help for social and charitable work. So she went to Delhi, which was said to be the fastest growing city in India, receiving as it did one hundred thousand immigrants a year.

Ranchi, Delhi, Jhansi became for the Sisters new fields of apostolate and the sign that the Lord wanted them to spread out through the whole of India. The work pattern for the new houses had been tested in Calcutta. The Sisters would bring the dying destitute to a haven of rest; they would take care of orphans, of crippled children. They would teach people to pray to God, organize Sunday schools, prepare children for the reception of the sacraments; they would visit the slums, teach poor girls crafts and prepare them for marriage and family life.

Mother was only too happy to start work in the capital. She soon received help from many quarters. Mr Cuttat, the Swiss Ambassador to New Delhi, an eminent scholar and devoted Catholic, was instrumental in obtaining his country's financial help for the foundation of a children's home.

Mother, who was generally considered to be a social worker interested mostly in bodies, in health and material well-being, took advantage of this occasion to show the Prime Minister that her primary concern was the spiritual welfare of the poor. A few days after this memorable occasion, she reported:

'The inauguration of our new Children's Home in Delhi was attended by Mr Nehru and the Swiss Ambassador. When the Prime Minister arrived, accompanied by Mr Krishna Menon, I said to them 'Let us first go and salute the Master of the house.'

'Then I led them into the chapel where I knelt in prayer. Mr Nehru, standing at the back, made a *pranam* with folded hands. Mr Krishna Menon went up to the altar to read an inscription and asked me its meaning. Then we went to sit on the grounds for the inaugural ceremony. The children garlanded the Prime Minister and offered him a spiritual bouquet. I explained that it meant that they had offered prayers and small sacrifices to God to obtain His graces for the Prime Minister. Then I asked 'Sir, shall I tell you about our work?' Mr Nehru answered me 'No, Mother, you need not tell me about your work, I know about it. That is why I have come.'

This simple, absolute word of praise was the finest acknowledgement of the services rendered to the poor of the country by Mother Teresa and the Missionaries of Charity. It came from the man who for seventeen years had spoken the mind of the people of India.

Bombay

Mother wished to open a house in Bombay, where she hoped to find good vocations among the large, fervent, well-educated Catholic community. This manufacturing city possessed many mills whose labour force lived in tenements, *chawls*; there would be plenty of work for the Sisters.

Bombay prides itself on being the premier city of India, the main centre of the country's trade and banking, the glamour city of cinema; it has a wonderful marine drive, rich villas and palatial mansions on Cumbala Hill. It is also the Indian town with the largest number of Catholics and the See of the first Indian Cardinal. The city has developed a large network of Catholic schools, colleges, social and charitable institutions.

'I have received invitations from several bishops,' Mother said, one, 'but no call has come from Bombay, though the Cardinal knows what we do.'

'Well, Mother,' I replied, 'you should not wait to be called. The Cardinal is an important person, a Prince of the Church; do not wait till he requests you. Offer him your services, he will accept, you will see.

Two weeks later, Mother was radiant:

'Father, I wrote to the Cardinal, just two lines to ask him if he would welcome us in his archdiocese. By return of post he answered that he would be very pleased for us to work in Bombay.'

Soon she was there, and Cardinal Gracias provided a house for the Sisters.

'He is very kind,' she said. 'He told me: I shall give you one of my best priests as a spiritual director for your Sisters.'

Mother soon returned to Bombay with a batch of Sisters and the work started.

At first, the people of Bombay frowned on Mother Teresa. She provoked their displeasure by remarking bluntly at the end of a short visit of inspection of the town: 'The slums of Bombay are worse even than the slums of Calcutta.' The Press was indignant, the people shocked by this quasi-blasphemy. Of course, Calcutta was known as dirty, rowdy, unkempt; but Bombay was the pride of India. How could this nun, after a few days in their city, pass such a sweeping and injurious judgement?

Mother silenced her critics. It did not take her long to size up a slum. She knew the criteria: light, water, garbage disposal, ventilation, air pollution, proximity to the market. In a matter of minutes she saw, weighed, compared, judged.

'The Calcutta slums', she replied, 'are mainly single-storied: fresh air enters into the dwellings, there is less congestion, more space for children to move about. Bombay is an island – its *chawls*, built close to the factories on scarce and expensive land, are three or four-storied; water has to be carried up several narrow flights of steps; ventilation is poor, the children have no open spaces for fresh air and games.'

The press soon réalised that Mother knew more about poverty than they did. Criticism gave way to respect. Still, the atmosphere would not be as friendly as that of Calcutta, at least for some time.

In November 1963 I was in Bombay to preach retreats to the diocesan clergy at the Bandra Retreat House. One morning, looking at the papers on the news-stands, a title struck my eyes: 'Woman found dead on Queen's Road'. A photo of the corpse which lay on the road for several hours was also published. The daily went on to deplore the shame of a city where a person could die on the street and remain there for hours before anyone came to remove the body.

During the retreats I spoke to the priests of apostolic charity and mentioned the wonderful work Mother Teresa's Missionaries of Charity were doing. At least in Calcutta the papers no longer reported cases of neglected destitute dying on the streets. The Church of Christ was showing to all what service of the Lord in his Brethren meant. The priests were visibly impressed. One of them came to me afterwards and said, 'I am in charge of a large parish. We have a house that is not used. Perhaps the Cardinal might allow me to offer it to Mother Teresa to open a home for the dying.'

Two weeks later, Mother said happily: 'Thank you, Father, you have helped us to obtain a house in Bombay. A parish priest has offered us a property where we can open a house for the dying.' It was quickly established, and became, as in Calcutta, one of the Sisters' most characteristic works.

The next year, the Eucharistic Congress took place in Bombay. The President of India, Dr Radhakrishnan, was there to receive the Holy Father. Pope Paul VI drove in triumph through the Bombay streets in a white Lincoln open car presented to him by an American benefactor. The popular enthusiasm cannot be described. Not thousands, but truly millions of people lined the fourteen mile route from the airport to the congress grounds; never in any country had such a crowd gathered for a reception to a Pope or for a Eucharistic Congress. In this very religious country, people belonging to all religions wanted to have a 'darshan' or spiritual glimpse of the great Holy Man of Christendom. They wished to see, listen to, come in contact with the most influential religious leader in the world. Wherever the Pope went, a huge mass of humanity surged forward to receive his blessings. Even among the organizers, no one had expected such demonstrations of respect and friendship.

The Pope had expressed a wish to visit some of the poorer quarters of Bombay, to meet at least a few slum-dwellers. It should not be said that he had come only for the well-to-do, in the land that had produced Mahatma Gandhi, the Father of the Nation, who travelled third class and journeyed extensively on foot. The Pope wished to show his interest in the poor and to approach them in their own houses. But the Civil Authorities quite rightly would not allow the Holy Father to move among the slum dwellers, followed by hundreds of reporters and photographers, of journalists and cameramen, who would have exposed to the eyes of the world the least attractive side of the country's life.

The Congress organizers solved the problem by taking the Pope to visit some charitable institutions. The Pope mixed freely with the children of an orphanage and delighted them by sharing their breakfast of buns and fruit; he showed his appreciation of the devoted work of those running this and similar houses.

Before leaving, the Pope donated his open white Lincoln car to Mother Teresa to be sold for her works. The occasion was acclaimed in the world press, which displayed photos of the Pope and Mother Teresa. Some of Mother's friends decided to raffle the car for her; they sold raffle tickets at one hundred rupees each, with the one single prize the car donated by the Pope. The sale of the tickets brought about four hundred and fifty thousand rupees for her charities. A non-Christian was the lucky winner.

Venezuela
Mother appeared to be thrilled as she said:
'We have been invited by a Bishop to go to Venezuela. Is that not wonderful?'
'Splendid, Mother. Where? Caracas?'

'No, not Caracas, a smaller place, not far away. This will be our first foundation in Latin America.'

We surveyed the great opportunities offered by the great continent which comprises nearly one half of the baptized Catholics of the whole world. There the Sisters would have real spiritual work, as much as they could cope with, among the millions of baptized Catholics who hardly practised their religion for lack of priests and nuns to instruct them and nourish their faith.

'Mother, you must make a big effort in that direction. Do accept every offer made by the bishops. Much can still be saved, preserved for Christ, but speed is essential. The Church loses adherents in South America every day, due to lack of spiritual care.'

Mother agreed: 'I shall send my best Sisters to start the new house.' She hoped to get vocations from the country itself, so that from Venezuela they could move into other South American countries. Soon, Mother was on her way to Venezuela. She would see her Sisters established, meet the Bishop, obtain help and collaboration from authorities and lay friends. In July 1965 the first foundation outside India was started. Mother came back delighted. The people were friendly, the Sisters had been well received.

This was only a start. Two more houses were established later in Venezuela. Then one in Lima, Peru. But the spread of the Congregation was slower than we had hoped. There was not the same enthusiasm as in India, though ten years later, at the beginning of 1975, she had requests from several bishops and made plans to open houses in Colombia, Bolivia and Brazil. The bishops were to discover what great help the Missionaries of Charity would bring them for the spiritual uplift of their poor.

Sister Dorothy, who had been Superior there and returned to Calcutta, reported: 'We were like deacons there. Generally the people are baptized; but many have never seen a priest or a Sister, due to the scarcity of priests and nuns in the country. So many people know nothing about Jesus. We had to teach them. We took communion to the sick. Eventually we administered Baptism. The poor live in *favelas*. We live in their midst. At first I could not understand them, as they only speak Spanish. But within two months I could manage. I learnt the language with the children's help. And some local girls joined us.'

'In Latin America,' said another Sister, 'we do much spiritual work. We do all that a priest here does, except hearing confession and consecrating the holy Eucharist. It is really wonderful work.'

Still, we had to acknowledge that the Missionaries of Charity had not spread there as fast as in India, as fast as we had hoped. Bishops and priests may not have realized their potentialities for the life of the Church. Their spirit and method, their personal, loving approach are well adapted to the needs of the downtrodden and spiritually neglected poor of Latin America.

The Sisters do not come with intellectual notions of conscientization, they do not worry about changing structures, or about opposing policies in the church. They go to the poor with the charity of Christ, with open hearts and hands. They speak to them a language they can understand. Their action is contagious and challenging – they obtain co-operation with the people among whom they work for their work. They bring a sense of respectability, of decency and self-respect to people who did not know them, did not realize that they count in God's eyes, have value for Christ.

Rome
Mother was radiant as she greeted me:

'Father, we have been invited to go to Rome. The Pope himself asked us to open a house there.'

A rare note of victory rang in her voice.

To Rome at the Holy Father's request; what an honour for a young Congregation. To Rome, like Peter and Paul. To her strong ecclesial sense Rome meant much; it was the heart and centre of Christianity, the See of the successor of St Peter, the Vicar of Christ on earth.

In a voice more subdued and thoughtful, Mother added: 'There is much work to be done, much poverty in Rome's suburbs; many people are in need of the Sacraments; many children do not learn their prayers; and there is much anti-God influence and propaganda. But we shall be close to the Holy Father; we shall work in the shadow of St Peter's.'

Mother did not need to reflect on this invitation nor to compare it with other possibilities. This was a sacred duty imposed by the Holy Father, who had befriended the community openly in Bombay. The Sisters would get ready as soon as possible, as soon as arrangements could be made.

To Rome the Sisters went, thrilled and joyful. They needed to show that they were not afraid of shouldering the cross of Christ. Romans knew more about virtue and vice, through centuries of experience, than any other city existing today.

To Rome had come countless saints – more were buried in Rome than in any other town; in Rome saints were officially proclaimed by the Catholic Church. But the Romans do not wait for any official proclamation to establish the fact of holiness. They discovered holiness behind appearances. When Benedict Labre, the Frenchman, who had come to Rome and for years lived in the porches of churches, neither washing much nor changing his clothes, eating whatever people gave him, passing his days in prayer to God, died, immediately the rumour spread through the whole of Rome: ' "Il Santo" is dead.'

When the Sisters were well established and fully at work, Mother spoke with special warmth of her Roman community.

'The Sisters are in a slum area; they live among the poor. They go to the market to beg for them. Everywhere they are well received. "The Indian Sisters" as the people call them, even though several of them are European, get chicken every day; at the market, the stall-holders give them, free, the less good portions which hotels and restaurants do not want. The Sisters teach the children their prayers and prepare them for the Sacraments. They visit the sick and old people in their houses.'

Thus the good work of the Sisters, backed by the prayers of many co-workers and of the sick and suffering, produces acts of love for God in Rome.

'The good works are links forming a chain of love around the world,' as Mother had prophetically written to her Belgian friend during the first days in the Upper Room.

To increase their Roman presence, Mother shifted the novitiate she had established in London to Rome. It was to receive the candidates from Europe and America, and also some from Africa. The postulants remained in London.

Australia

In June 1969, after holy Mass, a tall man introduced himself to me and asked: 'Could you do me a favour; I would like to meet Mother Teresa.' I introduced Mr McGee to Mother Teresa, who welcomed him.

He opened his briefcase, and pulled out a large bundle of notes, which he pushed across the table saying:

'Mother, this is to begin with.' Mother Teresa took the bundle, made no comment and started talking of the possibilities of apostolate among the poor in Australia.

Mother had paid her first visit to Australia in April 1969 at the invitation of Bishop Warren of Broken Hill, who wished her to start work among the aboriginals. So Mother and Mr McGee now made plans for this work. Knowing Ministers and officials as he did, he could help to get the required authorisation for the Sisters to establish themselves in his motherland.

John J. McGee's first visit to Mother laid the foundation for a most fruitful apostolate in Australia. He became a faithful friend of the Institute.

In the middle of September 1969, Mother went to Bourke with five Sisters to start their first foundation in Australia and to work among the aboriginals.

Mother was invited to Melbourne by Archbishop Knox who had known her in India. Some objected; in a country as rich as Australia, enjoying an advanced social legislation, surely there would be no work for her. There were no slums, no destitute, no people dying on the streets. Mother retorted: 'What, no work for us? And what about the habitual offenders when they come out of prison, what about their wives and children? What about the drug addicts, the alcoholics, are they not God's children in need of guidance and help?'

On the 26th April 1970 Mother Teresa and five Sisters left Madras by plane for Melbourne. They reached there the next day. Sister Monica was the Superior. The very first day, Mother, accompanied by the Provincial of the Loreto Sisters, found a house, and entered it. With the help of co-workers and students they cleaned the place. They started work immediately.

Sister Monica directed the Sisters to go on to the streets and discover the needy people. The Sisters came back, saying there were none on the streets. 'Then knock at the doors of houses' said the Superior. They did so, asking if there were any old person or persons in need in the house. At first people found them strange in their Indian dress. Also, they would not believe that they were nuns, wearing those strange habits. But the Sisters, by their kindness, gradually won their trust. They prepared the people for the sacraments and for the consecration of the families to the Sacred Heart of Jesus. They were helped and encouraged by some priests, and later by civic leaders who reported cases to them.

Their first big venture was to be a Home for the Rehabilitation of Alcoholics and Drug Addicts. In 1972 a plot of land was purchased in Greenvale and building started on the Convent and the Rehabilitation Centre.

Mother was invited to attend the Eucharistic Congress at Melbourne. There were three speakers only at the main session and Mother Teresa was one of them. She spoke on her favourite topic: her mission to serve Christ in the poor, to see the suffering Lord in his brethren in pain. Her words and her conviction moved the hearts of her listeners.

The Convent was blessed by Cardinal Knox in February, 1973.

Before departing in April, Mother Teresa left her Sisters with advice they remembered: 'I do not want you to perform miracles with unkindness, rather I prefer you to make mistakes in kindness.'

The Middle East

Mother was happy:

'Father, we are going to Jordan, in the Middle East; close to the birthplace of our Lord. The Sisters will be walking where our Lord walked and preached and worked miracles. Where our Lord died out of love for men. Is it not wonderful?'

Yes, this was truly good news. The Middle East was the cradle of the three great monotheistic religions: Judaism, Christianity and Islam, the religions followed by more than half the believers of the world. They were born in that rugged country, where man senses God's might and holiness. Abraham, Moses, were men of faith, as Mother was a woman of faith.

Christianity, starting from Jerusalem, had spread over the world in ever widening concentric circles; now it returned to its starting point through these nuns from the East.

In July 1970 the Sisters started work in Jordan.

In March 1973 they settled in the Gaza strip to alleviate the sufferings of the hundreds of thousands of refugees from Palestine. They were thus on both sides of the political frontiers.

Some time later, Mother expressed her happiness at spreading farther into the Middle East:

'We are going to Yemen, Father. We have been invited by the Prime Minister himself. After six centuries of Christian absence, with no priests in the country, no Mass, no Sacraments, there will be Mass again for the Sisters. After six hundred years! Is that not wonderful?

'The Prime Minister promised to do everything for the Sisters. He said, they should have no fear. He holds himself personally responsible for their safety. He guarantees that no one will cause them harm. His Government will give them every needed help and support. As a sign of good will be presented me with a "Sword of Honour" ' She laughed: 'A sword to me!'

'Yes, Mother, they are a martial race and good fighters, that is why they present you with a sword of honour.'

I thought too late of 'the double edge sword' that is the Word of God. That one the Sisters would have to wield – whilst bringing to all the peace so much esteemed in the East, the Peace of Christ.

Jordan
At the Mother-house, February 1976.

'Where do you come from, Sister?'

'I arrived from Jordan a few days ago. I am from Kerala, from the diocese of Trichur.'

'One of the best in the world for priestly and religious vocations. There is a wonderful spirit in your country. But now tell me about Jordan.'

'I was five years in Jordan, Father. I was sent there immediately after my first vows, at the end of the novitiate.'

'Did you come into contact with ministers or high officials of the Government?'

'No, we met only the poor.'

Here all glamour is absent, any feeling of being important and acknowledged as such. There is only the daily, humble, hard work, the contact with the very poor.

'What are your works there, Sister? Do you follow the same pattern as in Calcutta?'

'First, we work among the Catholics. Jordan has eight per cent Christians out of which two per cent are Catholics. We find them, teach the catechism, prepare the children for their first Communion. Then we visit the poor families, both Christian and Moslem. We give medicine to the sick. We have a home for the "unwanted", old people, mentally retarded, handicapped, abandoned children.

'We also go to the Jordan in a van given us by Caritas, and there we visit the sick.'

'What reception do you get?'

'The Moslems are quite friendly. They call us *Hajis*, because we wear white as they do when they go on pilgrimage to Mecca.'

'Do the women go to Mecca?'

'Yes, some go on pilgrimage. Of course the Moslems do not know what it is to be a nun; so they do not understand our kind of life. But they respect us.'

'At the beginning, how did you solve the language problem?'

'We had to learn Arabic. We were six Sisters; there are only five whilst I am absent. First we had a paid teacher. Then some local Sisters in Amman kindly volunteered to teach us.'

'Did you find the language difficult?'

'No. It is much easier than some of our Indian languages, say Tamil or Hindi. It has hardly any grammar. We learnt enough Arabic to be understood by the people.

'Our house is some distance from the capital. We hope to open a house in Amman itself soon. Then things will be easier; we shall not have to move about as much as we do now.

'You must one day have a Middle East Province or Region; can you hope to find vocations there?'

'Hardly; unless it be from among the girls we educate.'

'Did you receive the spiritual help you required?'

'There are very few Catholic priests in Jordan. In Amman, only two or three ministered to us. We could not find a priest for our annual retreat. Finally, we joined other groups of Sisters, and made our retreat with them.'

'And books? Do you have the spiritual books you need?'

'No, we are very short of religious books, especially good meditation books. Do send us some.'

'Yes, I shall try to help you. As you know, our Catholic Charitable Agencies provide food for the bodies of men, but less sustenance for their souls. That strikes many people in the much more spiritually-inclined East.'

'Your benefactors should also remember the spiritual needs of the Sisters.'

Yemen
At the Mother-house, February, 1976.

Two tertians have just arrived; one is from Kerala, one from Ranchi district. They have been in Yemen more than two years.

'What works do you do there, Sister?'

'We have a home for the unwanted, with 120 inmates. We have a handicraft class with a hundred students who learn sewing and various crafts. We have a dispensary.

'You should see the long queue of patients who come, often from far away. There have been up to six hundred in a single day. Now a hospital has been built close by, so we have fewer, but still two or three hundred a day. Sister Gertrude attends to them. They have a tremendous faith in her.'

'She was one of the first to join Mother.'

'Yes, the second, I think. She came from what is now Bangladesh. She is a doctor. She is very spiritual and has a wonderful way with the people. People come even from the Communist part of Yemen to consult her.'

'How are the officials? Do they help?'

'The Prime Minister is very sympathetic. He helps us in all ways. The Government officials also. They built our house. They asked us to give them a plan of a Catholic church, as they did not know how it should be built. They wanted to put up a church for our use. But we told them that we would use a room of our house as a chapel. If we used a big building, some might take it as a provocation. Many people are still very anti-Christian.

'The Prime Minister and the officials send us supplies. Twice a week they send us a pair of goats, so that the children and poor people may have good meat. They help us in every way. We had to open a second house, and they ask for a third.'

'Where are you established?'

'In Hodeida.'

'Can you go to the Communist part of Yemen?'

'People cross from one side to the other without difficulty. But we cannot go to Amman.'

'What about the work among the lepers?'

'It is wonderfully successful. At first I was frightened to go to the leper village. Have you seen Ben Hur? It was just like that. As in the days of Our Lord. We could hardly enter the village, because of the accumulated filth and rubbish blocking the way. We had to wade knee-deep through the filth. Then there were no houses. Only some sort of caverns cut out in the hills, into which people ran when they saw us approach. The women, completely covered by their *burkas,* hid themselves. Children ran for safety. The men were dishevelled, the children filthy. We called and waved to them, but they would not come. Slowly Sister Gertrude succeeded in establishing a few contacts. Gradually the people became accustomed to us and showed friendliness.

'For me, to go through the filth to reach the village proved an awful experience. But we had to change the ways of life of these people. With the help of Government officials we cleared the way, and removed the rubbish. Houses were built, gardens developed, flowers grown. We taught the women and children cleanliness, introduced some crafts for those able to work, to bring them respectability and make them feel useful.'

'Do you manage to prevent the children from contracting the disease?'

'When we arrived, nearly all of them were affected. Now, mainly through cleanliness and by isolating some cases, we hope to be able to protect the children.

'But the village has completely changed. Within two years, from a filthy spot it has become a garden village. The children sing the whole time. It is a real joy to go there. They love us and sing for joy.'

We remained silent for a while, thanking the Lord for the wonderful things He had deigned to do through His humble servants.

Seeing the spiritual results of their labours, the Sisters felt truly
enthusiastic about their vocation. They did not mention the
hardships of life, the harsh climate, the difficulty of adapting
oneself to a different tradition, culture, language, attitude to life.
They did it all for Jesus.

'Mother mentioned that a number of girls from the country
wanted to join you; what do you do about it?'

'Yes. You know, their parents arrange their marriage with
boys they have never met. Some of the girls do not like that.
Then, after coming in contact with us and seeing our religious
life, they want to live like us for God and for their neighbour.
Several girls told their parents they would not marry, but follow
our way of life. They would become Christians if they could and
enter religious life. But of course we have to be cautious, for
there might be a strong reaction from the families, endangering
our presence and work. So we let them come during the day and
work with us. For the night we send them home. They prove
most useful to us, for there is so much to do we could never
achieve it alone. We are only five Sisters.'

'Do you have a priest to minister to you spiritually? I believe
there are White Sisters and a couple of White Fathers.'

'Yes, the White Sisters reached Yemen a little before us. They
have opened a very good hospital. Now there is also a third congregation. Three White Fathers reside in the country; one, who
is a doctor, works in the hospital. Now we have Mass every day;
we did not have Mass daily at the beginning.'

'Do you hope to return to Yemen at the end of this year of tertianship?'

'Most certainly. I long to be back there and work again among
the lepers and hear the children sing and praise God.'

India: Coimbatore

This is a town in South India, which developed in an orderly
fashion, where some fifty middle size mills, most of them well
laid out, give employment to the local people. The place looks
prosperous and confident. The Bishop says he is invited and
welcomed everywhere, at every function organized by different
groups. An open society, unbigoted, forward looking. Also, a
centre of excellent coffee.

The Franciscan Missionaries of Mary, whose host I am, run three well patronized high schools. Their very well kept orphanage is a model of devoted and efficient medical care. The diocesan congregation of Sisters, fully active, also looks after the poor. This town does not seem to be a place where Mother Teresa's Sisters are specially needed. Still, the Bishop has invited them.

On the road I meet two Sisters in blue-bordered saree.

'Father, you do not recognize us?'

'Of course, I do. Can I come to say Mass for you?'

'Yes, the day after tomorrow. We shall come to fetch you.'

Two Sisters arrive at six a.m. We walk down the road.

'We shall take a bus. Let us wait here,' proposes one of the Sisters.

'But there is no bus stop,' I object.

'Never mind,' she replies. 'The drivers all know us and they stop anywhere to take us.'

And so it happens. A bus arrives, they wave to the driver. He stops to take us. He does not do this for anyone else on the way.

This makes me reflect: so these recently arrived Sisters have already struck the mind of the non-Christian drivers. They are not from the district, do not speak the language fluently, have no big institution; yet already it is accepted: they are for us, they work for us. The Sisters have established a personal relationship with these simple folk. They are closer to the people than other religious, who also spend their lives in work of charity.

'It is the same at the market,' says the Sister. 'Everyone knows us and helps us.'

We reach their house. In a verandah I see the emaciated faces of four persons lying on cots or mats, each covered with a blanket.

'They are close to death,' says a Sister.

Against the chapel wall stands the crucifix, and the call of Jesus dying is written: "I thirst!" I offer a Mass for the Sisters and a few children. I also tell them of the work God deigned to do through Mother Teresa, and of His love the Sisters must bring to the world.

After Mass, a Sister tells me: one of the old persons has died during the Mass.

We say a prayer, asking God to receive his soul in His love.

The Sisters then explained how they were gradually settling down, evaluating needs, finding out the possibilities for action. One typical problem; water was not easily available in sufficient quantity. It rains only five or six days a year in the area. For the children and the dispensary a good supply of fresh, clean water was absolutely needed and had to be found.

On my return to Calcutta, I told Mother that I had been to the new house at Coimbatore, and that this district gave many vocations to the Church.

'Yes, Father, that is why we opened a house there,' she answered.

Three years later one of the Sisters I had met at Coimbatore could report that their hopes were being fulfilled.

Already five novices and ten postulants had come from the district, who would be able later to work in places where there were few or no Catholics.

India: Mariapolli

'Mother, you are opening a house at Mariapolli?'

'Yes, Father. It is not a town and there are no slums, but to work in the villages is not against our Constitutions.'

She sounded apologetic.

'There are so many poor people in the area. We are also established at Takdah, which is not a town, and in Andhra Pradesh in some villages. We shall start with a dispensary; then see what the poor need most.'

On the Feast of Our Lady, Mother accompanied the first batch of Sisters to Mary's village, 'Mariapolli' in Bengali. Father Gabric had three buildings ready for them in the new mission station he had just started. It was truly pioneering work. For the sisters a chapel, a dispensary, a convent built with bricks were ready. The priest would live in a mud hut, for the present.

There was a nice teak wood *almirah*.

'Will this be for our medicines?' asked the Sister in charge.

'No, Sister,' replied Father Gabric, 'this is for your library of spiritual books, to protect them from the white ants.'

Father Gabric, who hails from Yugoslavia, is a priest after Mother's heart. He is the kind of person to whom Mother can refuse nothing; spiritual, austere, dynamic, habitually on the move, always ready to give something, visiting the villages, knowing every one of his parishioners and all the officials of the region. He exhorts his Catholics to pray and fast. He is often seen moving about with his beads in his hand. This helped him when he called on a Bishop in Australia.

'I went to visit a Bishop in Australia,' he recalled, 'and as I entered the room he was addressing a clergy meeting. "Look, Fathers," he exclaimed, "here is an old missionary from India who still believes in saying the Rosary. See, he prays to Our Lady even as he goes about." After that the bishop was ready to sign any cheque to pay for my new mission station.'

The Sisters started by opening a dispensary which proved to be an immediate success. Two hundred patients attended it daily. After a few weeks there were five hundred, and on some days even close to one thousand. People said: 'We come for the Sisters' prayers more than for medicine.'

Expansion goes on with increased momentum, in a cheerful, optimistic manner. The dynamic spirit of Pentecost continues to animate the Missionaries of Charity. New foundations were at first founded three a year, then five a year, and reached the number of twelve a year at the time of the Silver Jubilee.

'I wish to put seven or eight Sisters in each house,' confided Mother. 'This helps to keep up a cheerful spirit. Variety is good; more work can also be taken up.'

The new constitutions stipulate that each house should have at least six Sisters. In practice the initial number may be reduced to five or even four Sisters. Once needs have been estimated, activities can be diversified and expanded.

The geographical diffusion, helped by modern facilities, is probably unparalleled in the history of religious institutes. Starting from Calcutta, as their Jerusalem, the sisters went to five, ten, twenty different countries. They will soon be in fifty countries, and the novices who join now may one day be thrilled to count on the map one hundred countries where their society is at work for the glory of God. They will be happy, but not astonished; expansion is a fact of life for them. Often they have seen on the notice board: pray for our Sisters who leave tomorrow to open a house in Peru, Tanzania, Trinidad, Papua, Fiji.

A year after the Jubilee, even a book of five hundred pages could not describe adequately the genesis, preparation, establishment and first developments of all the new foundations. The few mentioned here indicate the main areas of development and tell of a few typical foundations in which the sisters work, and show God's hand guiding the Foundress and her Sisters.

In October 1976 a large map of the world was placed at the foot of the Crucifix standing in the staircase of the Mother-house, showing the various places where the members of the Congregation work for the poorest of the poor. Mother's dream has been realized; her Sisters form a chain of love for Christ and men, truly encircling the world.

7. In His Footsteps

'Take me for your model as I take Christ': St Paul's advice to the Corinthians.

First witness

'Sister Dorothy, you were one of the first to join Mother, you have known her well, what would you say is her main virtue? What struck you most in Mother's character?'

She thought for a while, and answered unhesitatingly:

'Her faith.'

'Sister, I would say exactly the same. The rock on which she has built her Institute and her whole organization is her faith in God. She is a woman of faith. She deserves the praise Elizabeth, moved by the Holy Spirit, bestowed on the Blessed Virgin Mary: "Happy are you because you believed." '

Like Abraham, the man of faith, Mother committed herself fully to God, accepted obedience to His order; sacrificed all she had, her religious congregation, her security, to put herself blindly in God's hands, not knowing what her fate would be. For her obedience in faith, God rewarded her as He promised to reward Abraham, saying:

'Because you have done this, I will shower blessings on you, I will make your descendants as many as the stars of heaven and the grains of sand on the seashore.' (*Gen. 22, 17*)

Her posterity on earth will be great, her posterity in heaven will be innumerable: the Sisters who came to her and all their spiritual children, those they helped 'to die with God', the children and adults they taught to know and love God.

Mother's faith and trust in God were never found wanting, being always alive and active.

'I take our Lord at his word,' she likes to say.

His word she finds in the Gospel, which she respects and obeys

87

as the inspired Word of God. 'Our Lord said it' is for her a final
argument. Thus she shows her faith in His person, His power,
His concern for her.

When Jesus said 'It is written', the argument was final; so
Mother says 'Jesus said', and holds fast to His word.

Second witness
'Father Van Exem, you have helped Mother from the very start;
tell me, what struck you most in her?'

'Besides her littleness, her trust in God.'

'Yes, the words of the Prophet Isaiah have proved fully true in
her case; "Those who trust in the Lord will renew their strength.
They will soar as with eagles' wings." ' (*Is. 40, 31*)

Her spiritual strength has gone on increasing with the years,
whilst her physical forces were renewed in a remarkable manner,
notwithstanding a hard life, repeated journeys on foot and by
train, lack of sleep, fever, trials, the care of a thousand Sisters.

Truly, she can say 'God has never let me down; my trust in
Him has never been misplaced.'

Yes, God knows his own and takes good care of them.

Once as we were talking in the small parlour, I said:

'Mother, you remember what our Lord told St Catherine of
Siena: "Take care of me and I shall take care of you." Well, you
have taken good care of Jesus and he has taken good care of you.'

'If it is for God's glory, Father, he will give us the means.'

She practices perfectly the advice of Jesus in the Sermon on the
Mount: 'Do not fret and worry about tomorrow. Your Father
knows what you need. If he feeds the sparrows, will he not much
more willingly give you good things if you ask him for them?'

Mother does not plan ahead; she allows God to guide her and
show what he wants her to do.

Her littleness, her sense of nothingness, strikes all who approach her and work with her. Perhaps it can be said that it
follows on her faith and trust in God.

She echoes the great mystics speaking of God and themselves as
'the Double Abyss', God's abyss of greatness, majesty and power,
man's abyss of littleness, misery and weakness.

By herself she can do nothing, but with Him she has power.
Power because she is His instrument. Her sense of being God's

instrument is extremely acute. Repeatedly she has said quite spontaneously:

'I am nothing. He is all. I do nothing of my own. He does it.'

One day, in 1975, she took a small pencil, about five centimetres long and holding it between her thumb and index finger, she said:

'See, that is what I am, God's pencil. A tiny bit of pencil with which he writes what he likes.'

Third witness

'Brother Michael, you have seen Mother at close quarters, tell me what struck you most in her character?'

'Two things I found remarkable in her, first her activity, then her smallness. Her activity is amazing. While others talk, she works. While others put questions, she solves problems. She has a sense of the real, of the urgent. She sees a need and fills it on the spot. An extremely practical person, she can take trouble to get things done.

'Then her littleness. She feels so humble, so insignificant in the hand of God. That is why it does not trouble her to be continually in the news, as she is now. She returns the glory to our Lord. All the good she does she attributes to Him.'

Her activity, her dynamism are of an exceptional richness and intensity. All her projects started to fill a need she had found. A man dies before a hospital, on the street: she seeks and opens a house for the dying. She sees abandoned children, she starts her Sishu Bhavan. A colony of lepers is expropriated, she goes into leprosy work in a big way. There is a famine somewhere, there are refugees to be looked after, immediately she arrives there with her personnel. She has a scheme, a programme; she organizes relief, begs for supplies, distributes help. Whether it be during the Bihar famine, the Bengal famine, the flight of nine or ten million refugees from Bangladesh, or later the earthquake in Guatemala, she is prepared to help. She must open a house in Papua because the people are very poor and the Bishop has no money – never mind, she will find the means.

She trains boys of the slums to make very simple pieces of furniture and sell them in the market. The Calcutta streets are littered in places with green coconut shells, she will organize people to gather them and make ropes our of the fibres. She has heard of an organization that rehabilitates lepers, trains them for some useful work; she too will open a house for that purpose.

She works fast; she is ready in a matter of weeks or months, not the years which some other religious societies may take to discuss conditions before opening new houses.

Essentially active by temperament, Mother Teresa cannot understand the long sessions at meetings where nothing or little happens.

'I was at a meeting of Superiors General in Europe,' she said. 'They talked only of changing the structures of society, organizing things in a different way. It all came to nothing; it did not do something for the poor, or preach Christ to those without religion, to those totally ignorant of God. I was happy when it was all over. They had insisted on my going there, but I felt like a fish out of water.'

Fourth witness

Brother Andrew, on his return from Saigon, stopped at Hazaribagh to meet the Australian Jesuits. I asked him:

'Brother Andrew, you have worked several years with Mother Teresa. You were caught by her ideal and you have successfully established the Missionary Brothers of Charity; may I ask you what impressed you most in Mother, during your long association with her?'

He remained thoughtful for a while. Then he answered:

'I suppose it is her singlemindedness. She has only one purpose.

'Mother also has a sense of humour; I think no one can be a Catholic if he takes himself too seriously. We must be aware of our inadequacy, our weakness, our nothingness before God.

'Mother works hard,' he continued. 'She sleeps little. Not more than two or three hours each night. I think she goes on writing letters till one or two in the morning. She always gets up at half past four.'

'Thank you, I shall remember that and try to imitate her singlemindedness.' Yes, she has one idea, one consuming passion. When we talk it is usually of Jesus and of 'the work'; for her the work is all to the glory of her Lord; she cares for nothing else.

Spiritually Mother Teresa resembles St Paul. Like Paul she is conscious of having been chosen by God the Father to work for the glory of Christ; to this end she founded her Society.

She has St Paul's passionate love for Christ and the Gospel. Like him she is Christ-intoxicated, entirely surrendered to Jesus and completely taken over by Him. With St Paul she can affirm 'Christ lives in me'. This presence of Christ acting in their souls has become for them a fact of experience. The truth, believed in faith, that by grace we become partakers of the divinity of Christ, who lives in the soul consecrated to Him, has become a matter of experience.

'Christ acts in me; he acts through me; he inspires me, directs me as his instrument.'

'I do nothing,' Mother likes to repeat. 'He does it all.'

When she speaks to non-Christians, *He* means God; when to Catholics, *He* means Jesus, to us she usually says Jesus, more intimate, more personal than the word Christ and showing her attachment to the person of Jesus. She likes to repeat that all is due to God who acts through her, inspires and sustains her. Thus she accepts no credit for any good effected through her. With St Paul, she can affirm without boasting: 'I live no more of my own life; Christ lives in me.' She knows it is not her weak frame, her limited capacity which turned the little headmistress of an obscure high school into the Superior General of a rapidly expanding religious congregation, and a world organizer of charitable works, hailed by the world press, praised by Pope and bishops, presidents and cabinet ministers.

Mother Terera mirrors St Paul in her faith, her reliance on God, her burning activity.

She shares his zeal, fearlessness, restlessness.

Both say, 'Preach only Christ and Christ crucified,' both are ready to suffer with him for the progress of the Church. Both are urged on by one thought and one passion; 'Christ crucified and risen'.

As St Paul says 'I rejoice in my suffering', so Mother asserts: 'We are happy to do this work'.

St Paul's vision embraced the whole world; he wished to proclaim the Gospel as far as possible. Mother from the start wished for a universal society that would work in every country, building a chain of love around the world. She has travelled more extensively than any religious founder ever before. She has opened houses in every continent, and sends her Sisters to as many countries as possible.

St Paul advises 'Treat everyone with equal kindness; never be condescending, but make real friends with the poor.' (*Rom. 12, 16*) Mother echoes: 'The poor make us the honour of allowing us to serve them.'

Like St Paul, Mother is shocked that Christ was not received by his own and is not received in the modern world. 'When I see how the poor remain neglected and unrecognized all around us,' she says, 'I understand the sadness of Christ at not being accepted by His own. Today those who ignore or reject the poor, ignore or reject Christ.'

When addressing the rich, Mother follows St Paul's advice to Timothy: 'Tell them that they are to do good, and be rich in good works, to be generous and willing to share – thus they will save up riches for the future if they want to make sure of the only real life.' (*Tim. 6, 18–19*)

And to the poor she says: 'Be satisfied with your condition, seek the better things, those that do not perish, are not eaten by moth or by rust, seek the Kingdom of God.'

To those completely surrendered to Him, Christ sends His Spirit in abundance; and the divine Spirit, says St Paul, brings them: 'love, joy, peace, patience, goodness, trustfulness, gentleness and self-control.' (*Col. 5, 22*) What a shower of wonderful gifts the Holy Spirit brings us. Love for God and men: true divine love animates those in whom the Spirit of love dwells. From love, joy blossoms as God, perfect bliss, brings joy to the soul in which He lives. Peace and harmony follow – we are united to God and friendly to all men. Joy and peace produce serenity, confidence that all God does is well done and that what He sends is for our greater good; as Mother tells her Sisters: 'Be happy, God loves you, especially when the work you do for Him is hard'.

Gentleness should lie in our relations with men, seeing in all of them God's image; kindness to all, treating them as we would Christ.

This requires self-control, since the spirit of Christ is opposed to the spirit of the world. And so St Paul adds 'You cannot belong to Christ unless you crucify all self-indulgent passions and desires.' (*Col. 5, 24*). Crucify; a harsh word – nail to the cross your selfishness, your vanity, your sensuality.

I found Mother habitually smiling, kind and increasingly serene, as the years went by. No doubt, the Spirit at times pours spiritual joy in her soul. But she has paid, she still pays the price of the souls she wants to save with Christ. The Spirit pours love, joy and peace into our hearts proportionately to our emptying ourselves of all self-indulgence, vanity, anger, ambition, and to our willingness to shoulder the cross of Christ. This is the price we must pay for spiritual happiness.

The Eucharist is the centre of the spiritual life of the Missionaries of Charity. The Eucharist as sacrifice, as food, as presence. In the Eucharist the Sisters find the strength, the inspiration and consolation that make their life both possible and meaningful.

With Christ they offer themselves as victims of the sacrifice of redemption to glorify God the Father. In Christ, received as a spiritual food, they find the strength to devote themselves unceasingly to all sufferers. To Christ, present in their midst, they come for advice, light, consolation. They keep Him company in his dereliction, quench His thirst for love.

The Cross of Christ and the words 'I thirst' face the Sisters as they enter the chapel – Jesus calls them, asks for their love, their service, their attention. They go down on their knees to adore Him, and then stay with their Lord, whether they are consoled or not; often they will feel like dry, parched land; they will suffer, as their Lord did at Gethsemane or on Calvary. 'I thirst,' says Jesus, and they understand His pleading: if they do not allay their beloved Lord's thirst, who will?

He is the Master, the Lord, the Friend, the Bridegroom, the divine Spouse to whom every one of them belongs body and soul.

They start the day by coming to the chapel for morning prayers, followed by meditation and Holy Mass. In the afternoon, the Sisters remain a whole hour in adoration of the Blessed Sacrament.

'I have no difficulty in believing in the real presence of our Lord in the Blessed Eucharist,' said Mother.

'Neither do most priests have any difficulty in that respect, Mother. What really tests our faith is the slow progress of the faith in Christ, the slow progress of His Church, the huge amount of sin and unbelief that remains in the world after nineteen centuries of redemptive grace, of the presence of Christ, of the heroic holiness of countless saints.'

Christ affirmed that He was present in the Eucharist when He said: 'Take and eat, this is my Body that will be given up for you; take and drink of this chalice of my blood that will be shed for you; do this in memory of me.'

The Fathers of the Church unanimously teach the reality of the presence of Christ. The Council of Trent declares most forcefully: 'Christ is present truly, really and substantially in the Eucharist.'

'Why then,' asked Mother, 'do some young priests shake the belief of our people by saying that, after the Mass, there is no real Presence in the Tabernacle? What do they teach them in some seminaries, nowadays? A newly ordained priest was sent here to give an instruction to the Sisters. I was present. The priest laughed at a number of our traditional beliefs; he said there was no need to genuflect before the Blessed Sacrament when you come to the chapel outside the time of Mass, for the presence of Christ was limited to the time of Mass and Communion. He also attacked the idea of religious obedience and ridiculed our traditional devotions. He spoke in that vein for a whole hour. When he had finished I led him to the door, thanked him and told him he need not come here any more.

'Then I returned to the hall and told the Sisters: "You have just heard what a young priest without experience said; they are his ideas and those of a small group. Now I shall tell you what is the traditional teaching of the Church." And for one hour I refuted all he had said.

'Mother, you did well. The Second Vatican Council reiterated the Christian belief, both Catholic and Orthodox, that Christ remains present under the Eucharistic species after the Mass, and that Christians should worship Him and visit their Lord present in the Eucharist in our churches and chapels.'

Mother firmly believes in the teaching of the Church, as entrusted by Jesus Christ to the supreme Magisterium: the Pope, and the Bishops united to him.

She obeys the precept of St Paul who said:

'You must live your whole life according to the Christ you have received — Jesus the Lord; you must be rooted in him and built on him and held firm by the faith you have been taught, and full of thanksgiving. Make sure that no one traps you and deprives you of your freedom by some second-hand, empty, rational philosophy based on the principles of this world instead of on Christ.' (*Col. 2, 6–8*)

Mother strongly believes that the Sacraments give us God's grace. They also indicate the proximity of Christ, who today acts in the world. The Gospel of St John, 'the spiritual Gospel' advocates worship in spirit and truth, giving little importance to structures and external rites, yet proves to be the most 'sacramental' of the four Gospels. Similarly, Mother's independent outlook and her dislike for structures do not affect her belief in the efficacy of the Sacraments instituted by Christ, nor her desire that as many as possible be helped to receive them.

This conviction fits in perfectly with her strong sense of instrumentality. We are God's instruments of sanctification for our brethren, whilst the Sacraments give grace, instruments used by Christ. She has also a peasant's respect for nature and matter which makes it easy for her to accept the signs established by Christ as signs of grace that all men can understand.

Mother strongly believes in the need for and efficacy of baptism; Christ told the apostles: 'Go and baptize in the name of the Father and of the Son and of the Holy Spirit.' For anyone who believes in God and his dispensation, baptism is neither a luxury, nor an optional practice.

'Father,' she said, 'I believe in the need for and efficacy of baptism. Some priests, imbued with modern ideas, tell me I am wrong; I answer them "Let's not argue. You will not convince me and I shall not convince you." So, we shall continue to baptize those who want to receive that Sacrament.

'Our best helpers,' she often says, 'are all the baptized poor who died and went straight to Heaven. Our best helpers are the forty thousand inmates of our homes for the dying who "died with God" after making an act of perfect love for him, surrendering fully to His holy will. They now pray for us and for our work; that is what brings so much grace to our apostolate.

'In Latin America many people have not seen a priest for several years, and so they ask the Sisters to baptize their young children; what a cause of happiness for the Sisters.'

Mother recalls with joy that tens of thousand Catholic children belonging to poor families have been prepared by the Sisters for their first confession and first Communion. They received their Lord in their simple and pure hearts. Some may not persevere in the practice of the faith, but at least they have received the good Lord in their childhood and that grace will always remain with them.

The new Constitutions stipulate: 'We take special care of the older children. We do our utmost to find out those who have not received the Sacraments and instruct them without delay.' Thus they will be prepared to receive the Sacraments of penance and the Eucharist; also baptism and confirmation if they have not received them.

Mother and her Sisters rejoice in seeing many marriages regularised and celebrated according to the rite of the Church. In Latin America especially, the Sisters have helped to sanctify thousands of unions of people who had not sought out or perhaps not found a priest to bless their union.

In one simple ceremony, said Mother, thirty marriages were celebrated by a Sister. In one case three successive generations received the grace of the Sacrament of Matrimony together, grandparents, parents and their children, a young couple.

Mother narrated with real happiness:

'In Rome, the Sisters are doing a wonderful job. They visit the houses of the poor; they wash and sweep, tidy, mend and cook for those unable to do so. They found an old man who must have been well off in earlier days. He lived all alone. As he was sick, the Sisters did all the work for him. One day he told them "Sisters, you have brought God here; now, bring the priest also." They brought a priest who heard his confession. The old man had not confessed his sins for sixty years. The next day he died in the peace of the Lord.'

Mother added:

'I told this story in the United States at a meeting they had asked me to address. After the meeting a priest came to me and said: 'I had decided to leave the priesthood and sent my letter of resignation to my Bishop. After hearing what you said, I shall cancel my resignation and remain at the service of souls as a priest of Christ.'

God's merciful ways proved too beautiful for words; we both kept quiet; this was truly the beginning of the joy of heaven: to behold God's splendour in His own light whilst bathing in His love. Mother's trust in God's divine providence never falters. Twice or thrice, with fifteen years' interval in between Mother described her attitude regarding money problems in exactly the same words.

'Money, Father, I never think of it. It always comes. The Lord sends it. We do His work; he provides the means. If He does not give us the means that shows that He does not want the work. So why worry?'

When Mr Thomas, the chairman of Hindustan Lever came to see Mother Teresa, to offer her a property in Bombay, he first asked her:

'Mother, how is your work financed?'

She answered him very gently:

'Mr Thomas, who sent you here?'

'I felt an urge inside me. . . .'

'Well, other people like you come to see me and say the same; that is my budget.'

It was clear: God sent you, Mr Thomas, as he sends Mr X., Mrs Y., Miss Z., and they provide the material means we need for our work. The grace of God is what moved you. God sees to our needs, as Jesus promised.

Her trust is as complete as ever. But it requires less of a foundation of faith, of belief in the words of Christ, than it did at the beginning. Faith was more needed, faith, namely belief in unseen things, as hope is the expectation of things not yet possessed, was more needed in the first dark years. After twenty-five years of the Institute, God's protection and help had become a thing of experience, a fact of life. It astonished no more, since it was always there. But it continued to warm and comfort the heart, whilst it called for never-ending gratitude. Mother could not possibly budget, that is, put down on paper her receipts and her spending for the year in advance. She could not foresee how

many Mr Thomases would appear during the year. It was God's
secret.

The Missionaries of Charity had benefited from the fact that
some multi-national companies had disposed of their unwanted
properties. These had shown the way to other companies. In
Calcutta, there was the *Prem Dan* of I.C.I., in Bombay there was
the *Asha Dan* of Hindustan Lever. Mother called them respective-
ly Gift of Love and Gift of Hope. Another Company might
provide later a *Viswas Dan*, a Gift of Faith; then the three
theological virtues would be represented. And one could foresee
a Gift of Grace, a Gift of Joy, a Gift of Friendship. As needs arose,
God would move the donors interiorly. They would be the first
beneficiaries of the gifts they made to God, by entrusting them to
the Sisters.

Mother has sparked off many acts of generosity. Various
organizations collect for her works. People want to donate.

'Where does Mother Teresa live?' people asked several times
after church service, or by telephone, or even on the street.

'I want to donate some money. How can I meet her?'

Of course, there may be the pleasant feeling of sharing in a noble enterprise, of taking part in a great adventure. One jumps on
the bandwagon of a true pioneer of a new era of practical charity. One enters into partnership with 'a living Saint'.

Mother is not affected by this psychology. If it helps the cause
of God and the welfare of the poor, good. But she considers
before all the spiritual value of the act of giving.

'I hope you are not giving of your surplus,' she tells a group of
rich businessmen who offer her a purse at the end of an excellent
dinner. 'You must give what costs you, make a sacrifice, go
without something you like, that your gift may have value
before God; then you will be truly brothers to the poor who are
deprived of even the things they need.'

The value of the act before God, not the amount of money
given her, that is her main concern. As a girl sodalist she learned
to make sacrifices for the missions, for the cause of Christ; to go
without a meal, to do without sweets or a new dress. She had
taught her Bengali pupils at St Mary's High School the same:
forgo a picture, an outing, a meal and give the money to the
poor. They did it, trained in self-giving until it hurts, and thus
they were prepared to assume the hardships of religious life on a

permanent basis, to love without limit the Lord Jesus and to take up the Cross with Him.

Money did not matter much; still, as good administrators of God's property, as stewards of God's gifts, they had to be faithful.

People who sent donations to the Missionaries of Charity knew that everything would be spent on the welfare of the poor.

At times it was the donors who were not sufficiently prudent.

'They steal my cheques,' Mother complained.

'Yes, such things happen. Foreign cheques, sent by post, are stolen and cashed in Hong Kong or in the Middle East. Have you lost many in that way?'

'I have informed my benefactors to send money only through bank drafts. But they do not always take this precaution.'

It was found that at least one hundred and fifty thousand rupees had been stolen from her; a man had even opened an account in her name and was signing for her in a bank located in Calcutta. But that fraud was discovered by the Security Department and the racket was stopped.

Money comes in from everywhere. Nineteen thousand pounds after the B.B.C. programme in 1975. The different prizes and awards were spent immediately on new foundations.

New foundations were started without debt, were paid for even before they were occupied. Benefactors have shown themselves extremely generous.

'We are opening a house at Nagpur,' says Mother. 'This is a town of a million inhabitants, with many cotton mills. The children's home and the house for the sisters are paid for by an Australian friend, fifty thousand in his currency. How many rupees does that make?'

'Five hundred and fifty thousand rupees, Mother.'

'Well, that is too much; the buildings cost only four hundred and fifty thousand rupees. May we use the rest of the money for another foundation, where the Bishop is very poor?'

At times the inviting Bishop provides the property and buildings. At times the Government makes all the arrangements. In Orissa, India, the Chief Minister, Mrs Satpathi, complained 'Why do you neglect our State, have you anything against us?' And soon the Missionaries of Charity opened a house there.

Once, on the feast-day of St Teresa of Avila, as I wished
Mother a happy feast, she laughed:

'I am not the great Teresa, I am the little Therese,' she said; 'she
is my patron.'

'No, I retorted, you are not the little Therese, who called
herself "the plaything of Jesus, the football of Jesus," you are not
the charming little Saint, who never left the four walls of her
convent and died courageously at the age of twenty-four. You
are Mother Teresa, a follower of the great Saint of Avila, always
ready to go out to start new foundations. For your Sisters you are
Mother; for us priests you are La Madre: a woman with an iron
will, dynamic and efficient.'

Spiritually, Mother is not a Carmelite. She follows St Francis,
the poor man of Assisi, and also St Vincent de Paul.

'In the plane from Madras to Calcutta,' she recalled: 'I spoke of
God to my neighbour, a gentleman I had never met. It was just
like meditating for the two hours of the journey.'

According to Indian spiritual usage the holy person, when
travelling, usually keeps quiet to apply himself to the contempla-
tion of the divine Presence. Everyone respects his silence and his
communion with God. Nor is there a better way to remind ordinary folk of the divine Reality to whom we are all going,
whom some know to be close to themselves. But for St Francis,
the joy of loving God and being loved by him deserved to be
told to the neighbouring traveller, who otherwise might remain
ignorant of it. So, when you travel, make your choice, edify by
your words, or by your silence. But I know what I would
recommend to the young nuns who have not yet reached the
sphere of perfect detachment from earthly things.

To imitate the perfect joy of St Francis in complete surrender
to God and full trust in his divine Majesty, such is the programme
of life Mother proposes to her Sisters.

Her spirituality owes much to St Francis. She emulates him in
the cult and practice of evangelical poverty, the love of the Cross
and the suffering Saviour, as also in obedience to God's guidance
expressed in the Scriptures. Like him she adopts a simple, unsophisticated approach to life and its problems.

Every day the Sisters recite St Francis' prayer, to obtain from
God kindness, gentleness, devotion, love and joy. They pray

'Lord, make me an instrument of your peace'. The prayer fits in
with Mother's idea of instrumentality. We are just 'God's pencil'
to write in the hearts of men what He wants. Like the Lord's
Prayer, this prayer has the advantage that it can be said by all
believers in God to whatever religion or denomination they
belong; they can pray it together, making a ring of love around
the world. It provides those who say it with a complete programme of life.

The kind of works the sisters perform and their style of life also
recall to mind the Daughters of Charity of St Vincent de Paul
and St Louise de Marillac. Vincent de Paul wished his Daughters
to visit the poor in their houses, at a time when nuns were
restricted to their enclosure and worked in their convents. He
sent out his Daughters of Charity to nurse the poor and sick at
home, carry food to the hungry, take care of orphans. They
dressed at first like French peasant women, and lived poorly and
austerely.

At times, Mother looked rather sad. Several times she
remarked:

'Father, we do so little. They praise us for our actions, but
what we do is not more than a drop of water in the ocean. It
hardly affects the immensity of human suffering.'

'You are right, Mother, but we are not divine providence.
You do all you can with the means and the personnel at your disposal. God does not ask you to do more.'

Indeed, the magnitude of human problems in several Asian
countries might discourage, if not appall. The Sisters may work
in twenty Calcutta slums, but an official estimate speaks of three
thousand slums in Calcutta. Then there are at least a hundred
thousand pavement dwellers. If the Sisters reach one hundred
thousand lepers, there are another two million in the country,
and also two million blind persons; and, according to an official
declaration of May 1976, three quarter of a million regular
beggars and vagrants.

Still, the work of the Sisters amounts to much. The Sisters
work, the Co-Workers are active, and a stimulus has been given
to the cause of charity all over the world among the millions
who read or heard about the Missionaries of Charity. We have

all become better for hearing of Mother and her Sisters and Brothers' love and devotion.

Again, Mother remarked:

'Father, our work among the slum children seems hopeless. When we succeed in educating a child, he goes to live in better surroundings and the slum people remain without any leader able to uplift them.'

On another occasion, Mother said somewhat sadly:

'Father, I do not build the Church.'

'No, Mother, perhaps not, but you are its best advertisement. You show the charity of Christ to all who come into contact with your institutions. And you have brought many children and adults to know Christ and receive the Sacraments they otherwise would not have received.'

'You see,' she said, 'we may not preach Christ as we would like to, because we receive help from the Government and from various agencies. So our hands are tied. You may preach because you receive no help from anybody. A government official told me: "Tell the truth, you would like me to become a Christian, you are praying for that?" I answered him: "When you possess something really good you wish your friends to share it with you. Now, I think that Christ is the best thing in the world and I would like all men to know Him and love Him as I do. But faith in Christ is a gift of God, who gives it to whom He likes." The gentleman went away satisfied.'

Mother has ever been a woman of action, indefatigable, always practical, concrete, quick to decide and implement her decisions. She brooks no delays, believes in today – yesterday, she says, is past, tomorrow is not under our control, it may never come, we have only today to be up and doing, to work for the glory of God.

She is a dynamo, an energizer, getting everybody to work. Whilst discussing matters of property with a government official, a Sister comes in and interrupts:

'An American tourist wants to see you; he is the person who came the other day.'

'Tell him to go and work in Kalighat.'

'But he says he went there yesterday.'

'Yes, he can go again today; the poor are still there.'
Another day I tell Mother:
'A lady would like to meet you.'
'No need. She can go and help. What can she do?'
'Well she runs a restaurant. I suppose she knows about catering.'
'We have no need of a caterer. Our meals are simple. Tell her to go and help at the dispensary. How many days a week can she spare?'
'I shall ask her.'
Many years ago Mother suggested:
'Father, you should write a book of meditations for my nuns.'
'No, Mother,' I replied, 'I cannot do it. I am not good enough.'
Some years later, she comes charging in again:
'Father, write a book of meditations for the Sisters. There are so few books of meditations adapted to the spiritual needs of the Sisters.'
'Mother, I cannot do it.'
Again, a few years later:
'Father, what about the book of meditations I asked you to write?'
'All right, Mother, I shall try.'
When my publisher a little later made the same request:
'No, I said, I cannot do it.'
But a week later I started writing meditations on the Gospel of St John. Inspiration came, and during a whole year I worked on this book – it was sheer delight. When the book was published, I sent one of the first copies to Mother.
She phoned me up a few days later:
'Father, thank you for writing "Remain in My Love". I use the book every day.'
I was repaid for all my efforts.

Mother's spiritual outlook has naturally progressed since the inception of her Congregation. Those of her generation who have remained in touch with her have noticed how her spirituality evolved during these thirty years, which was to be expected. She progressed in her understanding of the faith, of the ways of God's providence.

In Mother, with the passing of time and prayer, work, self-sacrifice, and a continual outpouring of love, the fruit of the Spirit has ripened and mellowed. In many of us, with age, as our physical arteries become sclerosed, so do our spiritual arteries. But this does not happen to those fully open to God's grace. The sap of divine life renews the arteries and the fruit of kindness becomes more fragrant and delicious.

Mother's faith and trust increased during the years; they gained in strength, naturalness, spontaneity, surfacing easily in conversation. Ingrained in the soul, they showed the reality of God's protection, his love always present.

At the Kalighat Home for the Dying, as a visitor wondered at the peace reigning in the last rest-house for the poor before their final departure, Mother said simply: 'God is here.' A concise, terse, perfect summing up of the situation. In earlier years she would have given a more elaborate explanation; now one word suffices: 'God' present, active, loving. In all matters, life's pattern appears simpler to her in God's increasingly stronger light.

Mother sees God active in these people as he prepares them for an eternity of happiness with Him. The ugliness of poverty and misery recedes into the background, as God's hand comes forward to receive His children whom the Sisters help to 'die with God'.

Serenity increases with age. Looking at the world from a greater height, we discover things those closer to earth cannot behold. We see how events fall in place to fit in God's plan; we realize that God is powerful enough to bring good even out of evil, if we let him do so. All serves to lead us to God, especially our sufferings, if we love Him. Suffering unites us to Christ, renders us similar to Him, brings merits, obtains grace.

Seen in the light of eternity, poverty, hunger and sickness shed their ugliness; they are seen as means helping us to reach God. Only sin is to be shunned – a worse evil than all the human suffering not caused by man. But to lighten man's burden on earth remains a sacred duty – to imitate the compassion of Christ for the multitudes that were as sheep without a shepherd, waiting to be led to good pastures.

Mother now would perhaps no more regret: 'We do so little; we do not build the Church, our action is like a drop of water in

the ocean.' She appreciates fully the sisters' call to collaborate
with God, to serve him in the poor, in a simple, humble way.

'Father, this is wonderful. . . .' Often she repeats this word of
praise of the Lord God who guides her. 'Wonderful' is the
qualification she uses most frequently when relating some event
or mentioning a favour received from God. In the spirit of St
Luke's Gospel she extols God's goodness, His providence caring
for His children, the grace and happiness of knowing and serving
Christ.

'They went away praising God' is Luke's usual comment after
narrating a miracle of Jesus. The ways of God really are wonderful; every spiritual person discovers the divine guidance in the
events of his life.

'How good God is', Mother likes to say, 'His guiding hand is
here'. It is. This renders her habitually optimistic.

Coming daily in contact with physical and mental suffering,
with misery, injustice, trampled-down human dignity, she suffers
from it, and tries to remedy the situation in a practical manner.
But she also sees all the good there is in the world: devotion, service, love, sharing, compassion, mercy, acceptance, gratitude,
good-will.

Camus, the author of *The Plague*, though an agnostic, thought
that in the world the sum total of goodness exceeds that of evil.
He could not give the reason for this. But a believer in God's
Providence and a disciple of Christ our Saviour can explain why
it is so.

8. Sharing His Cross

'Follow Christ by loving as he loved you, giving himself up in our place as a fragrant offering and a sacrifice to God.'

(*Eph. 5, 2*)

Mother knows suffering. She has shared in the Cross of Christ. Like every loving soul she would not wish it to be otherwise. 'We always find,' says St Teresa of Avila, who knew by personal experience, 'that those who are closest to Jesus have most to suffer.'

Mother puts before her nuns this ideal: to quench the thirst of Jesus crucified for souls. To do this they should be ready to suffer with Christ and even wish to be similar to Him and to suffer for the redemption of souls.

'The wounds I bear in my body are those of Christ' writes Paul; indeed, they are the wounds he suffered because he belonged to Christ. The Sisters, when they enter the chapel for their morning prayers, see the picture of the crucified Saviour, calling to them 'I thirst'. They will soon receive in communion the Victim of the sacrifice, who will give them strength to serve Him in the poor and suffering.

With Jesus they are to bring the world back to God our Father. This call brings them joy as they ponder Paul's words expressing the mystery of Christian love. 'It makes me happy to suffer for you, as I am suffering now, and in my own body to do what I can do to make up all that is lacking from the suffering of Christ for the sake of His body, the Church' (*Col. 1, 24*). In this process of redemption, as in everything connected with the existence and well-being of men, God wants our collaboration. We are to be His active instruments, sharing in His work.

Mother knows the suffering of men. How could she have true compassion without a sharing of experience, a 'symbiosis,' between those she cares for and herself. The sick understand the sick; the bereaved those who lose a loved one.

Mother has known fatigue, hard work, tiring walks, long waits; she has travelled in crowded trams and buses, she has sat up whole nights in cheap compartments; she has eaten rough food, and squatted on the floor with the poor in unfurnished dwellings.

'God made me a great gift: good health,' Mother told me. She has the hands of a peasant woman: strong, active, energetic, working and praying hands. She looks frail, increasingly so, as the years go by, but she is a bundle of energy. Her power comes from above: Christ is her spiritual power-house.

Like Paul she can be compared to an athlete perpetually in training, wishing to obtain the crown. With him she can say 'I treat my body hard and make it obey me' (*Cor. I, 9, 27*). Up at four-thirty every morning, she soon comes to the chapel for prayer. She goes to sleep late at night or even in the early morning. Sister Fabienne, who lives in the Mother-house, tells me: 'She works habitually till midnight or one in the morning.'

I always saw her sitting on the edge of her chair, her back erect, even when dog-tired, even when visibly feverish. When she is sick, it is difficult to get Mother to take some rest, still more so to keep her in bed. At times, Sister Agnes or a doctor has succeeded in forcing her to rest a little.

'I cannot ask Mother to come down today,' Sister Agnes said one day. 'She is not well. If I told her you were here, she would come down the two floors from her room and then climb up again. People come the whole day to see her. I must keep them away.'

'You are right, Sister Agnes. Look after Mother, protect her, give her the short rest she badly needs.'

She usually travels by train, in the lower class; she enjoys a free pass on the Indian Railways granted her by the Railway Minister. To spare her much time and fatigue, Indira Gandhi gave Mother a free pass for the Indian Airlines, in 1973. She can thus travel to all the important towns in India by plane.

Trials

Mother was deeply affected when some of the Sisters she had patiently formed and led to Jesus decided to leave the Congrega-

tion. Years ago, when she was asked: 'Do you lose many Sisters?'
she replied: 'Very few. In fact you could count those who have
left on the fingers of a single hand, and you would not even need
all the fingers.' It is so no more. With the considerable increase in
number of the Sisters, it must be expected that more will leave
the Congregation.

'Do you lose many Sisters?' I asked Mother after the Jubilee.

'No,' she answered, 'not many. Last year three left. The
Superior of one of our houses went away with the parish priest
who was the spiritual director of the convent. I went to see the
Archbishop of the place who told me he knew this priest had his
own ways. I answered him "Your Grace, if you knew he was not
reliable, why did you put him in charge of our Sisters?" '

But, if Adam proved weak, Eve was not altogether blameless.
She had been advised not to go alone to the parish house in the
evenings. As the Superior, she had not listened to her Sisters.

A senior Sister gave me a more complete picture of the losses
the Congregation had sustained during the previous year. 'Three
Sisters,' she said, 'left after their final profession. Nine more
Sisters left after their first profession.' These were free to leave at
the expiry of the period for which they had bound themselves by
vows. 'Danger,' added this Sister, 'comes from priests, drivers,
lepers, and co-workers. One Sister left to marry a leper she had
attended to; another left to marry the driver of the community's
van; still another left with a co-worker who had come to help
us.'

After the Jubilee Mother suffered a hard blow, when a Sister in
London who had been one of the pillars of the Congregation expressed the intention of leaving. Mother was so distressed that she
took the plane for London when she heard that this Sister, a
trusted and efficient helper on whom she had much relied, had
decided to leave the Congregation – perhaps on account of ill
health. Mother tried to make her change her mind, but failed.
Her magnetic power did not work. There remained only to
thank God for the good effected through this Sister, and to pray
for the spiritual well-being of those who had left the Congregation, as the Constitutions recommend in Mother's own
words:

'Pray for all those who have been in the Society that God may
protect them and keep them in His love.'

'We remain very human; we have our ups and downs,' Mother confessed several times.

'Yes, Mother, they keep us humble and make us feel the need of God's grace.'

Mother feels intense pain and immense sorrow when someone who has committed himself for life proves unfaithful to God's call and to his promise to live with Christ and to die for Him.

'How is it,' she asked, 'that nowadays all over the world so many priests and nuns abandon their calling? Were they not chosen by Christ? Did they not commit themselves to follow him after long and mature reflection? How then can a nun pronounce perpetual vows, and some years later give up the religious life? Are married people not bound to remain faithful to each other until death? Then, why should the same rule not apply to priests and nuns?

Mother suffers for her Lord, treated as an unwanted person, whilst His love is despised. Yes, someone will have to offer Him reparation for the faithlessness of those He had favoured with his call and His love, and who turned away after first following Him.

Mother has personally experienced that the Lord purifies us interiorly, in a subtle manner, depriving us of all spiritual consolations. Every loving soul must expect at times to be tried and deprived of all sensible consolation, of every feeling of God's sacred presence, as it is made to pass through the tunnel of the dark night.

In that *noche oscura*, as St John of the Cross calls it, that Dark Night known by all mystics and by many others, the marriage between God and the soul is being prepared.

Then those who out of a passionate love for God have left everything for Him – or perhaps not yet everything, since He asks still more from them – are heard to complain 'I have no faith; I work without faith, without feeling. Do I still believe? I see nothing.' They suffer with Christ in the Garden, with Christ on the Cross, sharing His apparent abandon by His Father, and exclaim: 'My God, my God, why have you abandoned me?'

To His chosen disciples Jesus says at some stage of life: 'From now on you must keep constantly before your mind: the Son of Man is to suffer. . . .' And with him they set their face deter-

minedly towards Jerusalem. Their pace does not slacken, their
faith in him does not weaken, as they show him their love by
sharing in the great act of redemption.

That grief and pain will also give way to the joy and serenity
of the Resurrection. Then perhaps, right at the end, or close to
the end of the road, the Lord will make the soul pass through a
final purification.

Setbacks

The Missionaries of Charity have experienced a few failures,
which is all to the good. Mother certainly thanks the good Lord
for them. Failures render us more similar to our Blessed Lord,
who failed with Judas; failed with the rich young man he invited to walk in his footsteps; failed to attract and convert most
of the priests and Pharisees of his nation. We should also experience that aspect of our Master's life: his disappointment at the
treatment meted out to God's prophets and even to His chosen
One. Still, the failures of the Missionaries of Charity have been
remarkably few.

There was Simla. The Sisters opened a house in that hill station. They came from the hot plains, the hills were very cold in
the winter; their clothing and style of life was not adapted to
cold days and nights; there being few Catholics in the area, the
opportunities for spiritual work were slender. The Sisters lost
heart, found their work useless and left the place. Yet they
remained at Darjeeling, which has a similar cold climate in the
winter, and flourished there; they went to Takda, as cold as Darjeeling, and more isolated. Such disappointments may depend on
the grit, determination, spirit of penance, enterprise and
enthusiasm of the first group.

Then there was Colombo. When Mother told me that the
Sisters had been invited to Sri Lanka, I asked her; 'Why is it that
other foreign religious have been asked to leave, whereas you are
invited by the Prime Minister to open a house?' Mother
answered: 'Ah, that is because we do what others don't do.' But
later the Missionaries of Charity were also asked to leave, and
they returned to India.

Belfast proved a more humiliating failure. Mother took four

Sisters there to open a house in 1972. The place offered a challenge: Protestants oppressed the Catholic minority, economically weak. Hatred was preached even from the church pulpits. Some Catholics in desperation retaliated with acts of terrorism. Mother was told: Here is a place for you, go and practise Catholic charity in Ulster; try to unite Protestants and Catholics through deeds of charity. Mother took up the challenge, in the spirit of St Francis going to the Holy Land occupied by the Moslems. Francis did get away with it, but the friars he sent a little later were soon despatched to enjoy the Beatific Vision in heaven. Their time of trial on earth ended with martyrdom.

The Missionaries of Charity did not die martyrs in Ulster, which would have covered them with glory and might have awakened world opinion. The Indian Sisters in their sarees had to pack and go home; they were not wanted.

What happened at Ranchi sounds less believable. As Mother arrived with some Sisters to open a new house, she was met with cries of 'Go back, Mother Teresa!'; she found a barricade erected on the road to prevent her going farther. Mother tried to argue, but in vain. The people were determined not to allow her to occupy the land bought for her new foundation. Mother told them 'By refusing entrance to the sisters you refuse entrance to God.' But this proved of no avail, and they had to turn back.

This was due to a misunderstanding, but also to a wrong choice of location. When doing good to the poor, we should respect the local people's interest and susceptibilities. Rumour had it that the new foundation was to be a home for lepers. The Sisters said it was not. It would be a house for the old and destitute. But the local people, who had built decent houses with their savings feared that a home for destitute would diminish the value of their properties and spoil the name of the locality.

A peaceful solution was found; the children's home established in another part of the town was shifted to the new property and the home for the dying destitute was moved to the old children's home.

Mother suffered a personal failure when she tried to settle a quarrel between the laity, some priests and the hierarchy. At Cuttack, Mother went to speak to the Catholics who opposed the appointment of a bishop; she spoke of the love of God, of faithfulness to mother Church, of our duties as Catholics, and of obedience to Our Lord, and they said they would stop their protest. The peace lasted a few days. Mother went back to her other duties, and soon the fight broke out again.

All this, and a little more, does not add up to much in the way of failures. Other religious founders have known much greater disappointments than this.

Other problems
Like St Paul, Mother experienced some trials on her journeys. One memorable incident happened on a hill-road. A terrible landslide had shocked Darjeeling, affecting a whole section of this hill station; the whole of Bhutia Basti had been destroyed, scores of houses had collapsed, some people had died, others, many of them, had been rendered homeless. It was the beginning of the monsoon and heavy rains had caused large chunks of earth to run down into the valley.

As soon as she heard of the plight of the people, Mother Teresa was on her way to Darjeeling to organize relief operations.

Then an accident happened. 'We were in the jeep,' recalled Bishop Eric Benjamin, 'the driver, myself and Mother Teresa, sitting on the front seats, and travelling on the old military road – for the regular road was blocked by several landslides. Suddenly, at a bend of the road, we were met by a lorry, and there was a head-on collision. The driver and myself, seeing the lorry come straight on us, steadied ourselves in order not to fall forward, and we escaped injury. Mother Teresa fell forward, her head went violently against a steel fixture attached to the windscreen, and she was badly cut. I noticed that she was bleeding under the saree that covered her head. She said it was nothing. But we returned immediately to Darjeeling and I took her to the Planters' Hospital where the doctor attended to her and put in nineteen stitches. Had the wound been a little lower she would have lost an eye.

'That very evening Indira Gandhi, who was in Darjeeling, hearing of Mother's accident, called on her at the hospital to express her sympathy and to convey her good wishes for a speedy recovery.'

A few days later Mother was back in Calcutta. When I met her at the Mother-house, she still appeared bruised and shaken. She smiled and said only: 'I am all right, Father.'

The Sisters also encountered dangerous animals. Dogs were not always friendly: A Sister at Raipur was bitten by an unknown small dog. She did not take the injections against rabies. For several weeks nothing happened to her. Then one day she was attacked by the dreaded disease. When she was brought to a Pasteur Institute and received anti-rabies injections, it was too late. She died; the Lord rest her soul and reward her for her good works.

At the Mother-house there was a terrible animal, a barker and a biter, aptly nicknamed by the Sisters 'Kala Shaitan', Black Devil. It was as fierce as a dog can be. It disturbed the classes and the study. Whilst I spoke on the Gospel of St John, the Black Devil would bark so loudly from its lair next to the hall that I had repeatedly to interrupt my instruction. One day, as I was leaving, it tried desperately to bite me, but I managed to escape its threatening jaws. A little later, it broke its chain and attacked Sister Camillus whom it bit in the leg, the arm and two other places. It had previously bitten Sister Fabienne who was in charge of the choir and a Sister in charge of novices. Then it bit a little novice in charge of nothing.

I suggested to some professed Sisters that the dog might be dispensed with; but they objected that Mother would be very sad; she loved Shaitan, who behaved like an angel towards her.

The Sisters also argued that Shaitan was to protect them against thieves. But a novice then told me, 'I live in fear and trembling of that dog, because I must cross the courtyard for my work in the evening, when Shaitan is let loose, and I am too small and weak to fight him back.'

It seemed to me that Shaitan had no right to disturb the peace and recollection of the novices, so I told this Sister: 'There is only one way out, we must pray the Lord to deliver us from this Black Devil.' Our prayers were heard sooner than we had expected.

A few days later two thieves came at night, and threw poisoned meat to the Black Devil. It ate the meat and became sick. The Sisters tried to save the animal, but their efforts failed. Kala

Shaitan had to be given an injection by the veterinary a few days later. The novices could now cross the courtyard without fear, even after dark.

9. Training the Sisters

'What do you think is our pride and our joy? You are; and you will be the crown of which we are proudest in the presence of our Lord Jesus when he comes; you are our pride and our joy.'

(*1 Thess. II, 19–20*)

Soon after the Jubilee, Michael Gomes said, 'Mother asked me lately, "Michael, do you know what is my most important work?" '

' "I suppose to work for the poor," ' I answered.

' "No," she said, "try again." '

'I tried to find the answer, and proposed several things. Each time she said "No, that is not the most important thing for me." Then she said: "Well, I shall tell you: my most important work is to train my Sisters." '

'Of course, Brother Michael,' I said, 'what could she do without the Sisters?'

'And what could they do without Mother?' he retorted.

'True, but she needs a team. She cannot run a single institution without the Sisters, who multiply and extend her influence. Mother knows that the Society will live after her only if the Sisters are fervent religious; she has told me so repeatedly.'

At first it was her main occupation. Now, due to her society's growth and expansion, Mother can devote less time to the essential work of formation, which she must entrust to the Sisters she trained.

Mother has to form Christ in the young candidates who come to join her Congregation. Like St Paul she can say 'My children! I must go through the pain of giving birth to you all over again, until Christ is formed in you.' (*Gal. 4, 19*).

For two years she watched over each new batch of novices, preparing them to become the chosen brides of Christ. She introduced them to spiritual life, abnegation, humility, service,

love of God and of their neighbour, and trained them to find
God in prayer.

Mother carefully prepares her young Sisters to become worthy
of their bridgegroom Jesus, so that their Lord may say when they
take their vows and pledge themselves to live only for him, to
serve only Him, to love only Him, to follow Him even unto
death on the Cross, in the words of the bridegroom of the *Song of
Songs*:

'You are wholly beautiful, my love, and without a blemish.'
These words the Catholic tradition applies to Our Lady. They
are an ideal we can aim at, an ideal put before the young
religious.

'If the Sisters are not to be faithful,' Mother told me, 'let the
Lord suppress the Institute. He can do without it, the Church can
do without it. They must be faithful to Him who has called
them, who is the ever faithful One.'

'Mother, they will be faithful.'

Having spared herself no pains for their training, to each of her
Sisters Mother can say with rightful pride 'I have betrothed you,
a chaste virgin, to Christ.'

'Father, I tell them: "You are the brides of Christ. He deserves
all your love. None of you must love Jesus less than a wife loves
her husband." '

'Yes, Mother, Jesus is the perfect Bridegroom, always faithful,
thoughtful, attentive to their needs, seeing to their spiritual
progress. But as a true lover, He is exacting. "I am a jealous
God" said Yahweh.'

'If they start seeking consolation in human things,' she added,
'if they divide their hearts between God and men, He may let
them fall.'

Mother teaches her Sisters by her example, and her words; she
guides them by her letters, and her visits to the various houses.

St Paul wrote to his disciples at Corinth, 'Take me for your
model, as I take Christ.' (*I Cor. 11, 1*) Mother can say the same to
her Sisters in all truth, without ostentation or self-praise. Indeed,
the Holy Spirit inspires the founders of approved religious
Institutes, whose members are expected to live according to the
ideal expressed in their Constitutions and their founders' life.

Mother can ask much because she has given much. She does

not ask the Sisters to do anything she has not done herself. She has washed feet, like Jesus; she has bathed sores and bandaged wounds like the good Samaritan; she has pressed babies to her heart as Christ did; she has lifted up the cripple. She has visited the slums; she has begged for the hungry and the sick. She has experienced hunger, thirst, tiredness: she has passed sleepless nights; she has had fever but still attended to her duties as Superior.

Mother constantly teaches the Sisters by her example. She arrived with five Sisters in Melbourne in April 1970. The same day, helped by the Provincial of the Loreto Nuns, she found a house which had been deserted after the death of the previous owner. It had been badly neglected, the roof was leaking, the floor covered with dirt. Mother announced: 'Well, we can start cleaning.' Immediately the front room was cleaned, prepared for Mass, and the beds were made ready. Since there was room for only five beds, one Sister slept under the table. Mother's arm had been fractured, and so the Sisters, to make her comfortable, disposed some blankets on one side of her bed that she might rest her arm.

When the night came, the Sisters soon fell into a sound sleep. On waking up, they discovered that the blankets had been spread over them to keep them warm during the cold night. Mother had seen to it; she could live in discomfort, like her Lord. No doubt, her action impressed the Sisters more than any instruction on charity could have done.

At the very beginning, the Sisters were hand-tooled; a carefully finished product coming from the hand of Mother, who spoke frequently to the several groups of Sisters.

'I give four of five instructions a day,' she could say at the time of the first foundations, 'and I meet personally every one of the Sisters.'

Gradually, as the number of houses increased, she had to rely more on her first companions. They were becoming seasoned and experienced; having imbibed Mother's thoughts, they transmitted her ideals and ideas, even using her favourite expressions. They were rightly exacting; candidates and novices had to be ready for a hard life under strict discipline. As Mother became more and more frequently absent, due to the opening of

new houses, the senior Sisters shouldered an increasing share of
the work of forming the postulants and novices.

From the start several priests also helped. Father Van Exem
contributed much to the Sisters' training, as the confessor and
spiritual director of the community in Calcttta. He helped to
mould the character of the Sisters in the spirit of the
Constitutions he explained to them.

Father Julien Henry also helped Mother in the spiritual formation of the novices and professed Sisters. He exerted a considerable influence on Mother and on the Sisters, stressing the
need for prayer, insisting on devotion to the Sacred Heart, the
Blessed Eucharist and to Our Lady. After twenty-eight years of
service to the Institute, he still gives an instruction daily to one or
another group of the Sisters.

'Father Henry,' said Mother with an impish smile, 'tells them
things no one else would dare tell them. He knows all their
defects and points them out in his instructions. When novices
spot him on the road, if they are not praying the rosary as they
are expected to do, they quickly reach for their beads and start
praying. But Father Henry has seen their gesture, and in his next
instruction he is certain to make them a remark. Nothing escapes
him, even though he himself, when alone on the road, usually
says his rosary.'

When they have left the Mother-house, Mother continues to
teach her Sisters through her letters. She directs, reproaches,
redresses, advices, suggests. She solves problems, encourages and
stimulates.

'I keep in touch with all the houses and all the Sisters,' she says.
'I visit them as often as I can; of course my visits become less frequent as the number of foundations increases. I also write often to
the Sisters.'

They are always present to her mind. Their problems are hers
to solve, their difficulties she must help to settle. She sends them
in the name of Christ whom she represents for them; hence she
must know whom to send where, whom to appoint as Superior of
the local community, what apostolate the Sisters should under-
take in a particular place. She goes to inspect the site of every
new foundation, by herself or with her counsellors. Once the
Sisters are established, she continues to guide them through her
letters and visits. She directs, encourages, reminds, corrects,

stimulates them in all religious and apostolic matters.

Sister Letitia, who later became the first Superior in Papua, when she was in charge of the house at Amravati wrote to Mother that the Bishop was giving the house two hundred rupees a month. Mother replied: 'Next month return the money to the Bishop and tell him you need this contribution no more. You must get the local people to help and support the work.'

At times she adds a note of humour to her advice, as when the Sisters from Dorunda, Ranchi, wrote to Mother that they could not sleep at night because thieves climbed the pipes along the walls of the house and tried to enter into the rooms were they slept.

'I wrote back,' chuckled Mother, 'since none of you is so pretty that a thief would want to take her away, they can be coming only for money and supplies. Well, allow them to take these things they need, and let the Sisters enjoy the sleep of the just. God will look after you.'

St Paul directed that his letters be read publicly to the assembled Christians, and then passed on to other communities. Mother's letters are also read in the community and travel from house to house. Many quotations from these letters have found their way into the second redaction of the Constitutions written in 1975.

A Belgian journal requested Father Van Exem to interview Mother, among other questions asked her was: 'What would you consider to be most important in the formation of nuns today?'

'What is most important,' Mother answered, 'is to train the Sisters to a deep, personal love for the Blessed Sacrament, so that they may find Jesus in the Eucharist; then they will go out and find Jesus in their neighbour, and they will serve him in the poor.'

This stress on the presence of Christ in the Eucharist and in one's neighbour as a key to spiritual training shows how concrete and incarnational her spirituality is: Christ is to be found on earth today, in definite conditions of time and space, in a truly tangible manner.

Thus the key-note of the training she imparts to her Sisters is Jesus found in the Eucharist, Jesus found in the neighbour.

The Eucharist is the Victim of the sacrifice to which the Sisters unite themselves, the sustaining Food that gives them the strength

to carry out their apostolate and the sacred Presence of their Lord
and Saviour, to whom they come to offer consolation and love,
and to receive inspiration and comfort.

Mother insists on prayer before the Blessed Sacrament, on
faithfulness to the hour of adoration every evening, which the
new Constitutions prescribe. Mother takes visitors to the chapel
and invites them to greet the Master of the house. She rejoices
when she learns that groups of her Co-Workers organize hours
of adoration.

This devotion to the Blessed Eucharist, fully in the tradition of
the Church, was again recommended by Vatican II.

Popular Indian tradition favours a concrete religion. But the
deeper current of Indian spirituality seeks God's presence in the
world and especially in the soul. The Sisters pass much time away
from their houses, since their work is largely outside. They spend
much time on the road or travelling. Thus, they must learn to
converse constantly with their Lord and to find God present
everywhere.

When speaking to the Tertians, I insisted on the divine
Presence within. Some of the Sisters understood this; some did
find God present in their soul and this discovery rendered their
prayer personal, intimate, habitual.

The one who loves Jesus will keep the two great com-
mandments: Love for God and for one's neighbour. Thus the
Sisters by their vocation are called to love, in a thorough and at
times a heroic manner. They discover God's presence, wonderful
inspiring, drawing the soul to Himself. With utter respect they
serve Him in their neighbour, as they tend the wounds of Christ's
suffering brothers and sisters.

Then the soul is itself a tabernacle. My Lord dwells always
with me, in me. Once as I spoke to Mother of the Presence of
God in the soul, she said: 'The indwelling? Yes, we have too
long neglected it.'

Like St Paul, Mother likes to feel close to the One she loves.
She sees the Eucharist as a continued Incarnation; she finds Christ
in the tabernacle and in His brethren; He is the Head, and they
and she constitute his Body. Christ in the tabernacle and in the
suffering poor expects the Sisters; they can visit Him and attend
on Him. Devotion to the Blessed Eucharist appeals to affective
souls, to those with a vivid imagination, to persons who like con-

crete things and situations. Several Sisters report that they find
strength to perform the day's work and shoulder its crosses in
their prayer before the Blessed Sacrament, telling Jesus in effect:
'Lord, take everything, all is for you.'

For her Sisters Mother has a high ideal.

'Father, I want to give saints to the Church.'

'Yes, you are right, Mother; to produce saints is the task of the
Church.'

And so she asks much and obtains much. She trains her Sisters·
to perfect obedience.

For Mother obedience means complete disponibility to Christ's
service, wherever and in whatever capacity he calls us. Like St
Francis of Assisi she asks from her religious perfect submission to
God's will as known through the order of the Superior, in a spirit
of love, and prompt execution of that will.

In the summer of 1968 there took place at Darjeeling the blessing and inauguration of a new building at the home for orphaned, crippled and handicapped children. The Bishop blessed the
new premises; the Governor of West Bengal praised the wonderful work performed by the Sisters. The Superior, who had
brought a difficult task to completion, might have thought of
relaxing for a while, but no – Mother Teresa, just back from
America and Europe, had news for her:

'Sister, I want you to go to Africa and start a new house there.'

'When, Mother?'

'As soon as you can obtain your passport. There is plenty of
work for us in Africa.'

Indeed after starting a first house in Tanzania, the Sister was
appointed to establish a second foundation in the same country.
This was a true acknowledgement of her pioneering ability.

To another Mother says:

'Sister, you leave for South India.'

'When, Mother?'

'This evening, Sister, by the first train that goes there.'

The Sisters are usually told of their assignment on the day they
take their vows, except for a few who require passports or visas
to go to their destination. When Mother is absent, they must
wait till she comes back.

'There is no problem of packing for us,' said a Sister. 'Since we have nothing, we are ready in ten minutes.'

The Sisters' training in poverty proceeds in a rigorous manner. They must not only know and esteem, but also experience practical poverty during their period of probation and during their whole religious life.

Poverty in dress which comprises:

A simple and modest white habit, covering them from neck to ankle and wrist.

A white saree with blue border to cover their head and most of their habit.

A crucifix hanging from the left shoulder.

Sandals.

They are allowed three habits: one to wear, one to wash, one to dry; and two sarees of coarse material, such as the poor would wear, one to wear and one to wash or dry.

The houses must exhibit poverty in style, in furniture; the manner of travelling must be the cheapest available: much is done on foot; when trams, buses or trains must be used, they choose the cheapest class.

Food should be of the most simple, yet sufficient to keep up the Sisters' health so that they can work strenuously for the good of the poor.

The Sisters sleep in dormitories, without any privacy, like the poor who live in crowded slums or tenements.

Cleanliness should be observed so as to give an example to the poor, who should be taught to work and not to be lazy.

The reason for the practice of poverty is love. Mother writes:

'Our people are poor by force, but our poverty is of our own choice. We want to be poor like Christ who, being rich, chose to be born and live and work among the poor.'

The Constitutions state: 'We and our poor will rely entirely on divine Providence. We are not ashamed to beg from door to door as members of Christ, who himself lived on alms during the public life and whom we serve in the sick and the poor.'

St Francis of Assisi was not ashamed to beg for the poor and to receive the scraps of food he would share with them. Similarly the Sisters are not to be ashamed to ask for the poor, even if begging represents a form of poverty that has come to be despised in the modern world.

The Sisters must learn to ask; they start doing it during their novitiate.

Two young novices come to the parish house, all smiles, and ask:

'Have you any candle drippings, Father?' Then both novices burst out laughing. They laugh and laugh heartily as only young girls can laugh. Who could refuse them?

'What do you need them for, Sisters?'

'To make a paschal candle.'

This is Passion Sunday. The two young novices went out early, gathered the children of a parish for the Sunday Mass and catechism class. On their way home they ask from other churches if there are drippings of wax with which they can make a paschal candle.

Another batch of novices went to ask for biscuits from a factory to prepare a treat for the children that they may share in the joy of the Resurrection of the Lord.

Bishops and government officials who invite Mother want her spirit, her approach to the poor and the abandoned, her way of work. Through the Sisters she has trained she can multiply her presence and her influence, her activity and her apostolate; they are the spirit and presence, the influence and work of Christ, living in his humble, docile, indomitable instrument.

Like Paul writing to the Corinthians he had nursed and formed into images of Christ, Mother can tell her Sisters: 'You are yourselves our letter that anybody can see and read, and it is plain that you are a letter from Christ, drawn up by us.' (II Cor. 3, 1–3)

The Sisters are to be a small replica of the foundress, modelled on her. In their behaviour and their work all men must see and read what Mother thinks and teaches and does. And because her spirit is truly the Spirit of Christ living in her, the Sisters are a letter from Christ, speaking to the world of His mercy, His goodness, His kindness, His power, His concern for every individual person.

Since Christ lives in them and acts through them, they should not fear to let the world see their good deeds.

'I tell them, Father, not to be ashamed when people praise them for what they do. They must let people see what Christ does through us, His humble instruments. It is all to His glory.'

'Yes, Mother; that is what Jesus told us: "Let your light shine before men that seeing your good works they may glorify your Father who is in heaven." Christ is the supreme Light, "the light that comes into the world to enlighten all men." He wishes us to be small lights, reflecting his truth, his splendour and glory.'

The Spirit of God grants the Sisters various charisms; it is for Mother to discover them, to help to develop them and to allow them to be used to the full.

At the Mother-house, I often saw a particular Sister speak to women and children on religious matters. As I mentioned this to Mother, she answered:

'Yes, this Sister has a special gift for contacting people and getting them interested in religion. She speaks to them of God with simplicity and conviction. Yet she only studied up to the eighth standard.'

'Well, Mother, if she has that God-given charism, use her entirely for that work. It is most important.'

'I shall,' said Mother.

Mother can ask much from her Sisters; but she also knows the limitations of human nature.

'I find it difficult to appoint a good mistress of novices,' she told me one day.

'You might try Sister X.; She is a woman of God, given to prayer.'

'No, she would be too strict. She exacts much for God and might break some of the young, weaker novices.'

In 1975, I asked Mother:

'Do you still know all the Sisters?'

'I know personally and individually every professed Sister of the Congregation,' she answered. 'But not all the novices and postulants.'

She judges them quickly. With correct insight, it would seem. Once, to test her knowledge of her Sisters, I asked her about a recently professed Sister.

'Where is Sister Y. at present?' If she knows the state of her soul, she will comment, I thought.

Mother answered: 'At our house at Z.' She added: 'she is a very spiritual person.'

'Yes,' I said, 'a very spiritual person.' We understood one

another. She knew that I knew, and I knew that she was aware of the treasure the Lord had given her.

Mother does not want mass production. There are nine separate groups of novices for the two years' novitiate at the Mother-house, with a Sister-in-charge to guide each group. Mother naturally puts her best Sisters to train the young candidates.

The novices do some field work, thus receiving in-training in the kinds of work they will have to perform later. The first year novices go out for work on Thursdays and Sundays. The second year novices go out for work every day except Thursdays.

Three points Mother stresses especially in the training of the sisters are:

Total surrender to God.

Loving trust.

Cheerfulness.

These three virtues must enable them to go through their religious life, coming closer and closer to the Lord Jesus whom they serve in the poor.

Each renovation of vows is preceded by a triduum of prayer during which the preacher is asked to take one of these subjects each day. Thus the nuns are prepared to give themselves again to God, to renew and perfect their offering to the divine Majesty in the spirit of the Congregation.

Cheerfulness in the fulfilment of the most unattractive task is a characteristic of the Institute. Mother teaches, and her words are inscribed in the Constitutions:

'Never let anything so fill you with pain or sorrow as to make you forget the joy of the risen Christ.' This is written at the top of the chapter on bearing the Cross of Christ, which is the proof of the greatness of His love and of ours in return for His.

Mother's faith has carried her through all the trials of the beginning of the Institute. Faith in the power of the Risen Christ and of the Holy Spirit He sent us will see the Sisters through all the difficulties of their life of service to the poorest of the poor.

Twice a year, on a feast day of Our Lady, takes place the ceremony of the vows. Those who have just finished their novitiate or are still juniors take temporary vows for a period of one year; those who end their tertianship, after six years of temporary vows, take their final profession, binding themselves for life to serve Christ in the Congregation. On these days Mother brings to Jesus the best offering she can make, the young religious she has carefully trained.

For the Sisters these are solemn occasions.

In December 1975, in crowded St Mary's Church, twelve Sisters were ranged in a single row before the altar; the Archbishop was going to concelebrate with twenty priests the holy Mass during which the Sisters would offer themselves for ever to Christ.

They were living the words of Hosea:

'I will betroth you to myself for ever, with integrity and justice, with tenderness and love;

'I will betroth you to myself with faithfulness and you will come to know Yahweh, your God.' (*Hosea 2, 21–22*)

It was their great day, long expected, long desired, long prepared. The day of their exchange of gifts with their bridegroom, Christ. They were coming forth in total surrender, joyful trust, perfect love.

The King who had called them to leave their families and every human attachment to serve him, had told them:

'Set me as a seal on your heart,
    as a seal on your arm.'

A seal to attest its owner's will – the seal that will guide and inspire her for ever, since 'Love is strong as death'.

After the Gospel and the homily, the deacon calls those to be professed, each one by her name:

'Sister Mary Edward.'

'Lord, you have called me,' answers the bride, acknowledging that her vocation is from God, not from men.

The celebrant asks:

'My dear Sister, what do you ask of God and his Church?'

'I ask that I may follow Christ my spouse and persevere in this religious community until death.'

The celebrant explains that this religious profession aims at the holiness of the nun who promises to follow Christ and work for the good of souls. By baptism they have already been consecrated to Christ; now they wish to be more closely united to him so that all they do and say, think and desire may be only for His glory.

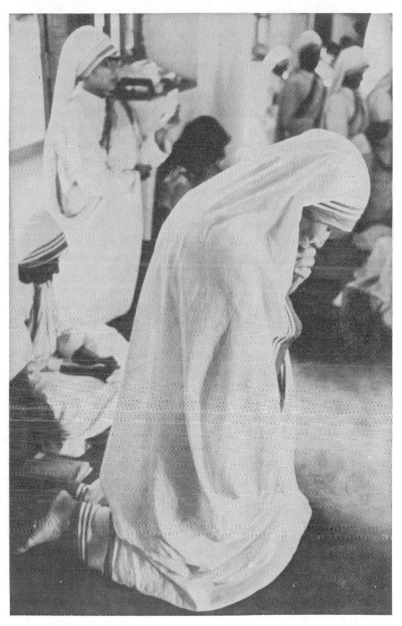

6. 'Immersed in God' – Mother Teresa in the chapel of
the mother house.

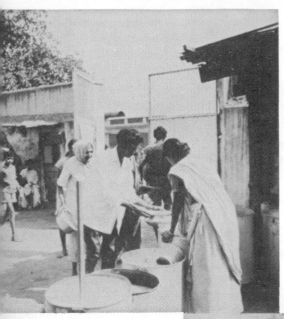

7. Food distribution in the courtyard of the mother house in Calcutta.

8. Clothing distribution outside a clinic in Calcutta.

9. Devotion and love – the young generation of
Missionaries of Charity.

10. June 1977 – Mother Teresa receives an honorary doctorate from the University of Cambridge. Behind her walks Mrs Ann Blaikie, Chairman in Britain of the Co-Workers of Mother Teresa.

'Dear Sister, are you resolved to unite yourself more closely to
Christ by the bond of perpetual profession'

'I am so resolved.'

'Are you resolved with the help of God's grace to follow the
life of perfect Chastity, Obedience and Poverty which Christ our
Lord and his Virgin Mother chose for themselves and to
persevere in it for, ever?'

'I am so resolved.'

'Are you resolved, by the grace of the Holy Spirit, to spend
your life in whole-hearted free service to God's poor?'

'I am so resolved.'

'Are you resolved to strive constantly for perfect love of God
and your neighbour by zealously following the Gospel and the
rule of this religious community?

'I am so resolved.'

The whole congregation then prays that they may be faithful
to God's calling and to their vows.

The Sister reads the formula of the vows, in which she says:

'I, Sister Mary Edward, vow for life Chastity, Poverty,
Obedience and whole-hearted free service to the poorest of the
poor according to the Constitutions of the Missionaries of Charity. I give myself with my whole heart to this religious community so that by the grace of the Holy Spirit and the help of the
Blessed Virgin Mary I may seek to practise perfect charity in the
service of God and the Church.'

The person who receives the vows then tells the Sister:

'By the authority entrusted to me, I accept your vows in the
name of the Church for the community of the Missionaries of
Charity. I commend you earnestly to God that you may fulfil
your dedication which is united to his Eucharistic Sacrifice.'

The newly professed goes to the altar, places on it the document of her profession which she has just read, and leaves it there
to be united to the offering of the Body and Blood of Christ.

She is to be a victim and a witness of God's love.

The celebrant proceeds to offer the Holy Sacrifice.

At the time of Communion, the words of Paul to the
Galatians, expressing his proud profession of faith are sung:

'I am nailed with Christ on the Cross; I live, not by my own
life, but Christ Lives in me!'

(II Gal. 19–20)

They belong entirely to Christ, they are ready to be sent out to any part of the world to do His work. They will go and integrate themselves into a community of the Missionaries of Charity, which, as their Constitutions direct, should by its fervour and active devotedness, radiate peace, joy and love.

10. The Brothers

> 'After this the Lord appointed seventy-two others and sent them out ahead of him, in pairs, to all the towns and places he himself was to visit.'
>
> (*Luke 10, 1*)

'Behind Bishop's College in Ahiripukur Second Lane,' Mother said one day, 'the Sisters have discovered a group of Catholics who do not seem to be known by the parish. Nobody goes to Church and the children have not made their first Communion. Several unions are irregular. The Sisters would like to regularize a few marriages. The same happens in other slum areas; we discover people who were not married in the church and yet live together. The Sisters try to obtain the information and documents required to regularize the situation of these people. When dispensations are required, parish priests do not always prove very helpful. I need one or two sympathetic priests to work with the Sisters; they would visit the slums and co-operate with them. Then we could do more spiritual good.'

I quite understood their predicament. The prescriptions of Canon Law had to be followed. Some matrimonial situations were intricate. As happens in every large city, people came to Calcutta in search of a job, leaving a wife or husband at home, and then settled down with another person to cook and keep house for them. Children were born out of wedlock. We all tried to help these innocent children. Mother said she needed sympathetic priests to help her Sisters, visit families with them and settle cases. She seemed to throw out an invitation.

But I told her I was not her man, as I had a full time job as Professor of Economics. Mother foresaw many difficulties in the way of a man visiting the slums when the menfolk were out at work, and only the women and children were at home. That would hardly be tolerated. The man would be suspected and unwelcome.

One or two priests did try the experiment of slum work with
the Sisters. But Mother had larger plans. She was considering a
new foundation: a Congregation of Brothers, similar to that of
her Sisters, trained in the same spirit, working together with
them.

The beginnings of the Missionary Brothers of Charity proved
more laborious and less successful than that of the Sisters. But
Mother's perseverance prevailed. The Church does not favour,
even does not allow a woman to be the head of a religious congregation of men. So Mother Teresa had to find a suitable priest
or brother to direct the new Institute and launch it into being.
Divine providence sent her the required person, a Jesuit, author
of several books and booklets presenting the Catholic faith to
non-Christians, and destined to work at the Catholic Enquiry
Centre of Poona and the Institute for Home Studies. He was
Father Ian Travers-Ball, an Australian Jesuit, then making his tertianship.

The tertianship brings to an end and crowns the long religious,
philosophical and theological training of a Jesuit, with ten or at
least several months of prayer, study, reflection and experiments
conducive to spiritual development and to discovering the will of
God for his religious. Father Travers-Ball made it with zest and
zeal. He felt the call of God to work with Mother Teresa, in the
same spirit, to work among the poorest of the poor in the slums,
among the most needy and abandoned. He received all encouragement from his religious Superiors and from his brother
Jesuits. All rejoiced at seeing one of their own help to develop
the family of the Missionaries of Charity by opening its male
branch.

Mother Teresa was delighted, as she saw God truly bless her
work. She could not expect better than a fully trained religious
priest, young and dynamic, experienced in the religious life.

Some years later the Congregation of Brothers had grown, and
I had a chance to learn more of their work.

In September 1975, I chanced to meet Brother Andrew, the
bearded Superior General of the Missionary Brothers of Charity,
who had just arrived in India from Saigon.

'I was not exactly expelled from Vietnam,' he said, 'but the
Communists took away the three houses we had and occupied

them. With no possibility of work, of starting anything, and no place wherein to reside, I took the plane for Bangkok and India.'

He had previously sent home to the United States four American Brothers and also a Brother from the Netherlands; the Americans would have been in danger at the time the Communists troops entered Saigon.

Three Indian Brothers had already returned to India from Cambodia. One American postulant refused to leave when the Khmer Rouges entered the city where he was working. The last that was seen of him – and that was five months before we spoke – was that he was marched away by soldiers from the Cathedral Square.

'I am going to write a book on Mother Teresa and the Missionaries of Charity,' I told Brother Andrew.

'Yes,' he answered, 'by all means do it. Tell them that we are very ordinary people, that God does everything. You must "demythologize" what has been written about us, and what many people think of us.'

He hesitated before pronouncing the word 'demythologize'; as a theologian, he knew its ugly undertones. He was aware of the harm some religious theories had done to the faith of many, by tearing off and discarding all the miraculous elements in the Gospels. But he used the word, and repeated it without any sign of regret.

'You must demythologize what has been written about us and our work. No doubt much good has been done to a large number of readers by what has appeared. But we have to spend at least six months trying to correct the wrong ideas of the candidates who come to join our Congregation after reading some of the things published about us.

'You must say that we are very ordinary people, all of us. We have our defects, our foibles, our shortcomings, the Sisters as well as the Brothers, even Mother Teresa. She and I do disagree and at times we quarrel. We are instruments inadequate to the task. But the marvellous thing is that God uses us for his work and has produced through the Institute a tremendous amount of good.'

Brother Andrew spoke in the true Christian spirit, as Scripture says: 'To you, Lord, not to us, to you be the glory.' And when we labour for him in that spirit, the Lord does work marvels through his grace.

Brother Andrew stressed the point, as he must have done often when speaking to his young Brothers: the glamour of being in the public eye is dangerous and may do us harm. He had just experienced true poverty and had been forced into complete detachment: of his three years of exertions in Cambodia and Vietnam to establish his Congregation, what remained? Of the Brothers' work, of their efforts to help people, what were the results? Nothing visible – only a few acts of love of God made in faith, which had value for eternity.

Then we spoke of the very beginnings of the Missionary Brothers of Charity. I asked him:

'What influence did Mother exercise on you and your decision? Did she ask you to join her?'

'No, the decision was entirely my own. It just happened. It took very little time. It was during my tertianship at Sitagarha, near Hazaribagh. I had always been interested in the poor and wondered what I could do for them. During my tertianship, I was sent as an experiment to work with the Brothers residing at Sishu Bhavan for a few weeks. When I returned to Sitagarha, I spoke to Father Schillebeeckx, our instructor. I told him I wanted to join the Brothers. He immediately agreed. The Calcutta Jesuit Provincial approved the plan. Permission was asked from Rome to allow me temporary exclaustration. Within weeks this permission was granted, and I left immediately for Calcutta to join the Brothers. All the Jesuits were most encouraging and co-operative.'

'Was the Brother's Congregation already established then.'

'No. There were a few candidates: but Rome did not approve the foundation, though the approbation was requested by Archbishop Albert D'Souza and by Mother. Rome answered: 'First get more candidates, then we shall approve you.' This was a vicious circle; no approbation meant few candidates, since priests would not send us candidates as long as we were not a recognised Institute, but recognition by Rome depended on larger numbers. We explained the matter and finally Rome granted us recognition.'

'Who was in charge when you joined?'

'When I joined them, the few candidates were being trained by Mother and Father Julien Henry. I am afraid they did not relish being under a woman Superior.'

'Neither does Rome allow congregations of priests and brothers to be ruled by women.'

'Soon we got a house in Kidderpore and we started on our own.'

'Did Mother have much influence on the training of the Brothers?'

'Well, we disagreed on some points. We had some arguments.'

He hid his face behind his hands, and added: 'There is a letter not to be published as long as one of us is alive.'

Out of discretion I did not enquire further about the cause of their disagreement. Had not St Paul quarrelled with John Mark who refused to follow him? When later Barnabas proposed that they take Mark with them, Paul refused and 'after a violent quarrel they parted company, and Barnabas sailed off with John Mark.' (Acts 15, 39) This quarrel puts in the shade the disagreement between Mother and Brother Andrew.

Of course the Brotherhood was first Mother's brain child, the product of her efforts, her prayers and her financial backing. For many years the brothers would be known by the public as 'Mother Teresa's Brothers'. Indeed, they are the Missionary Brothers of Charity, having the same name as the Sisters.

'How many Brothers do you have at present?' I asked.

'The Brothers number about one hundred and fifty. We have already opened fourteen houses, in Calcutta, Titaghur, Noorpur, Midnapore, Bokaro, etc. They started in Los Angeles, where two of the four American Brothers speak Spanish. The Cardinal gave them a house which serves as a novitiate.

'In India vocations have come mainly from Chota Nagpur and Kerala; a few came from Bengal, Tamil Nadu, Bombay and other regions. Some candidates joined us from the U.S. and other Western countries.'

'It will be more difficult to recruit and train the Brothers than the Sisters,' I commented.

'I am glad you recognize the fact,' said Brother Andrew.

The life of the Brothers is not easy; it asks for much self-denial and a deep spirit of prayer.

The percentage of Brothers dropping out during their training is much higher than that of the Sisters. As Brother Ferdinand stated: 'We were thirteen in my year of novitiate in 1967; at the

end of two years training seven remained to take their vows. In
1975, for our final profession, we were only four to bind ourselves for life to the Institute.'

'What are your main works, Brother Andrew?' I asked.

'We try not to go where the Sisters are working. But we
collaborate with them wherever it is useful. We share the work
with them at the Kalighat Home for the Dying. We look after
the men whilst they take the women's ward. The Brothers also
take care of some destitute sick who are not too ill or weak, in
one of our houses. We look after orphaned, abandoned and
crippled boys. Many of the Brothers work among lepers. In
villages and small towns the lepers are much neglected. The
Brothers have assumed this apostolate in earnest; they render
very valuable service in this field.'

'Yes, you have here a rich field of apostolic service, calling for
genuine Christian self-denial, devotion and true love.'

The Brothers took charge of the Titaghur hospital for lepers
after the Sisters had experienced some difficulties in dealing with
the men. This specialization should attract to the Brothers good
vocations and rich blessings from heaven. Indeed, several
Brothers, including Brother Sebastian, the Master of Novices,
who is a priest, felt attracted by this apostolate and applied to join
the Missionary Brothers of Charity.

Whilst Brother Andrew, the Superior General, was away in
Vietnam, Brother Ferdinand was chosen to be his Vicar in India,
and he still occupies this post. This allows Brother Andrew to
travel about more freely and organize new foundations abroad.
He does not intend to bring to India candidates and novices from
Western countries to train them in the Indian manner. He thinks
that living conditions are too different, whereas Mother at first
brought to Calcutta all her foreign candidates. She started
novitiates in Melbourne and Rome only when she found it
difficult or impossible to obtain visas for her foreign candidates.

Girls may be more resilient and adaptable than boys. Still,
Brother Andrew may be right in adapting the Brothers' training
and life style to local conditions. His Jesuit formation prepared
him to follow the example of St Ignatius, a founder of genius,
who told his religious to adopt the language, culture, and style of
life of the people to whom they ministered. The Brothers have

no distinctive habit; they dress simply and wear a cross pinned to their shirt or coat as a sign of their religious consecration.

The Society counts five priests among its members. Some joined it as priests. As a rule no candidate is admitted specially for the priesthood; it is left to the Society to decide who will be sent to study for the priesthood. It does help the Brothers to have priests among their own members, since this allows them to open houses in mission areas without priests or church.

The Missionary Brothers of Charity, who share Mother Teresa's universal outlook and concern for the souls of poor and suffering children and adults, at present look eastward and plan to open houses in Taiwan, Hongkong, South Korea. They will expand as much as their resources in personnel allow. In this they depend on God's providence; but prospects for recruitment seem fairly good. The future progress of the Congregation will depend mostly on the solidity and depth of the spiritual formation of the young Brothers.

11. The Helpers

'You are God's chosen race, his saints; he loves you, and you should be clothed in sincere compassion, in kindness and humility, gentleness and patience.'

(*Col. 3, 12*)

'I have three Second Selves,' said Mother.

Indeed she has her own, inalienable self, then she considers as her Second Self in the Congregation Sister Agnes, who replaces her when she is out of Calcutta. She has of course, her spiritual Self, her innermost Self, the Lord Jesus living in her by his grace. Completely surrendered to Jesus, she allows him to take over her direction and act through her.

'I have three Second Selves directing groups of helpers, who work on behalf of our Institute. These form three branches: the Co-Workers or Coadjutors, the Sick and Suffering and the Contemplatives.

'The co-workers are directed by Mrs Ann Blaikie in England. They are forty thousand lay persons. Fourteen thousand in the U.K., six thousand in the U.S., some in Belgium, France, Australia, and so on. They meet regularly; they pray for us; they also prepare bandages and clothes, and other things we need for the dispensaries, for poor children. What matters is that they work for God. In several places they have started organizing holy hours for our work; they have meditation, prayer.'

The material aspect had little importance for Mother; it was only a way of showing one's love for God in action. That they prayed for her work delighted Mother's heart. For this woman of God, money counted little and material services were unimportant, if they did not proceed from love of God.

For a while we remained silent, thanking the Lord for this auspicious development.

'Then,' Mother continued, 'there are the Sick and Suffering, seven hundred of them, I think, organized by Miss Jacqueline de Decker, my Second Self. She worked for some time in India. Now she is in Belgium. She underwent seventeen operations. Some time ago she wrote to me:

' "You are going to receive a great favour from our Lord, because of late my pains have increased." She offers her sufferings for the work of the Missionaries of Charity. Miss de Decker has organized several hundred sick persons who also offer their pains for the success of the Sisters' work.'

'My third Second Self,' said Mother, 'is a French priest, Father Georges Gorrée, who organizes the wing of the Contemplatives who support the Missionaries of Charity by their prayers and penances.'

'Have you houses in France?'

'No,' she said sadly. 'We have not been asked.'

'I quite understand. The present French attitude, mainly among priests and religious, may be too sophisticated for your simple approach to religious and charitable work. But some bishop will probably call you before long.'

'Do write to my three Second Selves,' concluded Mother, 'they will provide you with information for your book on our Institute.'

The Sick and Suffering

The Sick and Suffering was the first link to be organized and connected with the Missionaries of Charity. The idea and initiative came from Mother herself and in the first years of the Institute. She felt acutely that prayer and sacrifices were needed to obtain graces for the apostolate of the Sisters. She felt like St Paul, writing: 'I beg you, brothers, by our Lord Jesus Christ and the love of the Spirit, to help me through my dangers by praying to God for me,' (*Rom. 15, 30*) and repeatedly asking for prayers in his letters to his new converts.

Mother had met Jacqueline de Decker at the Patna Holy Family Hospital where she stayed after leaving her Loreto Convent. Miss de Decker wished to work with Mother and join her religious Institute, but her ill health would not permit it and she was forced to return to Belgium after a stay of two years in India.

Miss de Decker kindly sent me copies of letters Mother wrote to her during the heroic first years, the years of blind faith and trust in God. These hitherto unpublished letters, written with complete openness to a kindred soul, reveal Mother Teresa's ideals, aims, and feelings at the start of her new vocation as no other document does. The letters were written in the Upper Room, in the spirit of the Cenacle. For the history of the beginnings of the Missionaries of Charity they provide an invaluable source of information.

Mother asks the support of Miss de Decker's prayers and suffering. Very early she wished to organize a 'wing' of Sick and Suffering persons to help her fledgling Institute.

In October 1952 Mother Teresa wrote from the Upper Room at Creek Lane to Jacqueline de Decker:

'Today I am going to tell you something which I am sure will make you very happy. . . . Why not become spiritually bound to our Society? While we work in the slums, etc, you share in the merit, the prayers and the work with your sufferings and prayers. The work is tremendous and I need workers, it is true, but I need souls like yours to pray and suffer for the work. Would you like to become my sister' – Mother had first written 'child' but crossed out the word and wrote above it 'sister' – 'and become a Missionary of Charity, in Belgium in body, but in soul in India, in the world, where there are souls longing for Our Lord; but for want of someone to pay the debt for them, they cannot move towards Him. You will be a true Missionary of Charity and you will pay their debt, while the Sisters – your sisters – help them to come to God, in body.' Here Mother echoes the words of St Paul: 'I fulfil in my body what is lacking in the sufferings of Christ for His Body, the Church.'

Mother continues: 'Pray over this and let me know what is your desire. I need many people like you – who would join the Society like this – for I want to have:
1. 'A Glorious Society in heaven.
2. 'The Suffering Society on earth – the Spiritual children.
3. 'And the Militant Society; the Sisters on the battle-field.

'I am sure you would be very happy to see the Sisters – fighting the devil in the field of souls. They count nothing as too hard when there is a question of souls.'

Then Mother adds a remark that will comfort all those who suffer with peace and joy: 'Our Lord must love you much to give you so great a part in his suffering. You are the happy one, for you are His chosen one. Be brave and cheerful and offer much for me — that I may bring many souls to God. Once you come in touch with souls, the thirst grows daily.' Mother again stresses that what moves her to action is the welfare of souls she wants to help to know, love and serve God.

In January 1953 Mother writes and explains further the function of the Sick and Suffering: 'I am happy you are willing to join the Suffering members of the Missionaries of Charity; you and all the sick and suffering will share in all our prayers and works and whatever we do for souls, and you do the same with us your prayers and sufferings.

'You see, the aim of the Society is to satiate the thirst of Jesus on the Cross for the love of souls, by working for the salvation and sanctification of the poor in the slums. Who could do better than you and the others who suffer like you Your suffering and prayers will be the chalice in which we the working members will pour the love of souls we gather around. Therefore you are just as important and necessary as we are for the fulfilment of our aim — to satiate the thirst of Jesus we must be a chalice, and you and the others, men, women, children, old and young, poor and rich are welcome to make the chalice.' Mother does not discriminate between persons; everyone is invited to help, to contribute whatever he can in the matter of love for Christ.

But there must be unity of purpose among all the members, who should be animated by a common spirit. Mother specifies that they should show forth the three characteristic virtues of the Missionaries of Charity:

'One thing we must have in common is the spirit of our Society: total surrender to God, loving trust and perfect cheerfulness.

'Everyone and anyone who wishes to become a Missionary of Charity is welcome, but I want especially the paralysed, the crippled, the incurables to join, for they will bring many souls to the feet of Jesus.' Again Mother stresses that her aim is to lead souls to Jesus; to achieve this end prayer, work, suffering offered to God are needed. Thus started the link of the Sick and Suffering that was to help the work of the Missionaries of Charity.

In March 1955 Mother writes to the Sick and Suffering: 'Every day we offer you or rather offer each other to Christ for souls.

We, the Missionaries of Charity, how grateful we must be – you suffer and we work. We finish in each other what is wanting in Christ.' Here Mother again refers to the Paulinian idea of our collaboration with Christ in his Passion for the good of souls. She adds:

'What a beautiful vocation is ours: to be carriers of Christ's love in the slums. . . . We stand together holding the same chalice and so with the adoring Angels satiate Christ's thirst for souls.

'My very dear children, let us love Jesus with our whole heart and soul. Let us bring Him many souls.' Mother indicates again her main purpose, namely to bring souls to Christ who thirsts for them, who offered himself as a sacrificial Victim to reconcile them to his Father.

She ends with her usual advice: 'Keep smiling. Smile at Jesus in your suffering – for to be a real M.C. you must be a cheerful victim.' She echoes the words of St Paul: 'God likes a cheerful giver,' and 'I rejoice in my sufferings.'

Mother ends with words reminiscent of the Last Supper: 'How happy I am to have you all. You belong to me as much as every Sister belongs to me here.' The Father to whom the Sick and Suffering belong has entrusted them to Mother that she may offer them to Christ for whose glory they were created and now labour. 'Often when the work is very hard, I think of each one of you, and tell God "Look at my suffering children and for their love bless this work" and it works immediately. So you see you are our treasure house.'

In another letter Mother explains what is for her 'the Way of Love': 'Very often I come to you in my thoughts and offer your great sufferings when my own are small or nothing. When it is very hard for you, just hide yourself in the Sacred Heart, and there my heart with you will find all the strength and love which He chooses for you.

'What a beautiful vocation is yours: a Missionary of Charity – a carrier of God's love; we carry on our body and soul the love of an infinite, thirsty God; and we – you and I and all our dear Sisters and the Sick and Suffering will satiate that burning thirst – you with your untold suffering, we with hard labour; but are we not all the same — one "As you Father in me and I in you" said Jesus. You have learned much, you have tasted the chalice of His agony . . . and what will be your reward More and more suffering and a deeper likeness to Him on the Cross. When you pray, ask Jesus to draw me closer to himself on the cross that there we may be one.'

Mother shares St Francis' idea of the 'perfect joy' on earth: the soul reaches this fullness of joy when she accepts to suffer for Christ, and even asks to be united to his Passion, so that the Master and his loving disciple may be more perfectly similar.

Mother feels specially attached to her Sick and Suffering Brothers and Sisters, similar as they are to Christ their Head who suffered for the redemption of mankind. She considers their help to her work invaluable.

The Co-Workers

'The organisation of the Co-Workers,' writes Mrs Ann Blaikie, 'started in a haphazard way when I approached a friend in 1954 to find out if she knew whether Mother Teresa could be approached, as I thought that among our European friends we could collect enough toys for her annual Christmas party, about which we had read in the Calcutta press. (I was living in Calcutta at the time.) Without delay we met Mother Teresa and proposed our plan. She was delighted, and asked us whether we could raise enough money for her to buy dresses or shirts and shoes for her Christian children at Christmas. This we were able to do. After Christmas, Mother came and saw us and asked if we were able to raise sufficient money for the Muslim children's annual festival! After this, of course, we realized that she would be asking us for the Hindu children's party, and so we were, as they say, "hooked".

'We called our small group of women the Marian Society, as it had been started in the Marian Year, and we did, of course, also work for many of the Catholic missions. Soon we spread out and were joined by Indian ladies and other non-Europeans.

'Mother Teresa then asked us to take over the money-raising for her leprosy work, and this we also did. Then gradually groups of women formed small working parties to roll bandages and to make paper bags for the lepers' pills.

'In 1960 several of us who had belonged to the original group left India and returned to England. The good Lord saw to it that we settled within ten miles of each other and it was only a week after my arrival in England that I was caught up again in the work of Mother Teresa by John Southworth, the chairman of a leprosy relief charity. He had been sending money to Mother Teresa and she told him to contact me as I could give him first hand information on the work. About six months later Mother Teresa passed through London and appeared on television, and from that small beginning the U.K. branch of the Co-Workers was born. John Southworth was its chairman, I was its vice-chairman and our other ex-India friends in Surrey, formed the committee.

'We based our work on prayer and on giving our members an opportunity for service; people knitted or rolled bandages, collected old clothes and either sent them to India, or sold them and sent the money. But always we emphasised that it was the love that was put into the doing that was important rather than the amount of money raised.

'Some four or five years later Mother Teresa saw the poverty in London and asked her Co-Workers to help those in need in their own neighbourhoods; this is the development which is spreading through the country. Co-Workers now work in geriatric hospitals, with the mentally handicapped, with lonely old people and with others.

'Our prayer life, too, has developed, and hours of prayer among the Co-Workers are now held in very many towns and villages. The one in this village is held in the home of a Co-Worker who is a link with the Sick and Suffering. She is an arthritic in a wheelchair, and her husband is an epileptic. We meet with them once a month and pray with them, and meditate on the prayer of the Co-Workers. Day and week-end retreats are also held around the country. All our prayer activities are on an ecumenical basis, as Co-Workers are of all denominations and religions.

'Similar work is being carried on in other countries where there are branches of Co-Workers. Some countries started when nationals returned to their countries and formed groups. Others started spontaneously, as for example, in Ireland.

'Some have started because a Sister from the country joined the Order, and her friends supported her, and still others have been moved by the publicity about Mother and the Missionaries of Charity to write in and ask what they could do to help. Then after a year or so they have become branches of the International Association. We have Co-Workers also where there is no official association, and these we keep in touch with through our International Newsletters. We have Co-Workers in Poland and Hungary, and as far as Japan and with the Eskimos in the Arctic Circle.'

Thus the Co-Workers have penetrated where the Sisters have not yet entered.

'Our Co-Workers' way of life,' Mrs Blaikie explained, 'is a way of love, seeing Christ in everyone and ministering to Christ in that person. The Missionaries of Charity take a fourth vow, that of wholehearted free service to Christ in His most distressing disguise and it is this which we as Co-Workers must carry on in our lives. Mother Teresa bases the life of the Co-Workers on prayer. The daily prayer of the Co-Workers is the daily prayer of the Brothers and Sisters. Our meetings start with the prayer and then two or three minutes of meditation. She also asks her Co-Workers to join together for an hour of prayer once a month.

'The Co-Worker then goes to show his love for his family, for those in his street and in his neighbourhood, in his country, and in the whole world, seeking out the lonely, the handicapped, the sick and the old, the bereaved and the abandoned, bringing the love of Christ to them.'

On the 26th of March 1969 the International Association of Co-Workers of Mother Teresa was affiliated to the Congregation of the Missionaries of Charity, and their constitutions were blessed by Pope Paul VI.

The link with the Contemplatives

Father Gorrée writes from France: 'In September 1974, as she travelled through France, Mother Teresa expressed her wish that all the houses of her Missionaries of Charity be adopted spiritually by one or several convents of contemplative nuns. Mother asked me to organize this spiritual twinning on an international level.'

Father Gorrée willingly accepted responsibility for this 'linking up' of active Sisters and contemplative nuns in various countries. He approached a large number of contemplative congregations and found a ready response among many of them. Soon he could contact the houses of the Missionaries of Charity and inform them that 'Contemplative nuns have accepted to offer to God the Father their prayers and sacrifices in union with those of His Son Jesus Christ, to obtain the graces that will render their apostolate fruitful.'

The twin communities were asked to send news of their respective work, apostolate, and spiritual experience to one another, so that by knowing each other better they might both be stimulated to serve God more generously.

The result has been remarkable. Within a year, close to four hundred monasteries in Belgium, Canada, France, Germany, Italy, Luxemburg, England and some other countries had with joy and enthusiasm accepted to be linked spiritually to a house of the Missionaries of Charity. An exchange of news and letters started; prayers, sacrifices and work were offered reciprocally for one another.

What struck the organizer of this spiritual twinning most is the joy that it caused among the Sisters of both communities. This feeling for Co-Workers we have never seen nor spoken to is a manifestation of the charity the Holy Spirit pours into our souls.

The Spirit Christ sent us brings joy in abundance. This is the joy Christ promised his disciples at the Last Supper, when he said: 'Remain in my Love . . . so that my joy may be in you and your joy may be complete.' (*John 15, 9–11*). This is the joy of the Risen Christ, the joy of the messianic era that has begun, the joy that the Spirit of Love, the Spirit of Holiness pours into the souls of the disciples inasmuch as they are surrendered to Christ who lives in them.

The Contemplatives are on the mountain with Christ alone in prayer to His Father, sometimes in the morning, sometimes in the evening, at times even the whole night. They are reserved entirely for the service of God, interceding for the needs of the Church and the sanctification of men, whilst the Missionaries of Charity, in the field, work for the salvation and sanctification of the very poor, those cherished children of God.

Thus Christian charity stretches out over the oceans, beyond all barriers, all frontiers of language, culture, nationality. United two by two, each team a link of a strong chain encircling the world to the praise and honour of the infinite God.

12. Publicity

Mother Teresa's success owes much to her remarkable ability to obtain collaboration from every side. She enlisted the help of the Pope, of prime ministers, chief ministers, presidents of various states, and a considerable number of laymen.

She also used all the modern means of mass communication. The media made her known and thus rendered her work possible. They made her first a state, then a national, and finally a world figure. Without the help of the press, the radio and television, her activities would have developed only slowly and would probably have remained confined to India.

'The Statesman,' a leading Calcutta daily, was the first to throw a spotlight on her by mentioning her in its columns. 'The Amrita Bazar Patrika,' another leading daily, followed suit.

English and American dailies spread her fame abroad: *Time* mentioned her several times and carried her photo.

In 1975, *The Illustrated Weekly*, the weekly magazine most widely read by the middle and upper classes in India, displayed Mother Teresa's picture on the cover. In the main story the editor, Kushwant Singh, praised the work of the Missionaries of Charity.

Some months later, in August, Mother told me: 'Mr Kushwant Singh's article has changed the people's attitude towards us. I notice the difference: there are no more misgivings or frowns when we are mentioned. All show sympathy and appreciation for our work. This is really marvellous.'

Mother added: 'Kushwant Singh wrote to me – he wished to make me meet other newspaper editors when I go to Bombay, so that I may talk to them of the poor and of their responsibilities to the weaker members of society. He ends with the words 'God bless you,' she added with a chuckle, 'though I think he is not a believer.'

'I gave a B.B.C. interview,' recalled Mother. 'Malcolm
Muggeridge had asked me to appear on one of his programmes.
That was the first time I appeared on T.V. They received me at
the studio and led me into a small room with a table and two
chairs. I sat on one of the chairs and started saying my rosary.
After some time, Mr Muggeridge arrived, sat down in front of
me, and started asking me questions. He had a paper with a list of
questions before him. He read two of them which I answered;
then I went on talking about what I wanted to say.'

Naturally, his prepared questions dealt with her and the
history of her work. As usual, Mother did not want to speak of
herself, but of God. It was all God's work. He did it, not she.
Malcolm Muggeridge, a good journalist and interviewer, was
conquered by the personality, the dynamism, the energy, the
faith of the woman sitting before him. Still, it was unusual to see
a Catholic nun in religious habit lead an experienced writer and
producer to the subject she wanted to develop. She would make
the public hear about God, his love and power. They would be
told of the love of Christ which alone motivated these Sisters to
devote their whole lives to the service of their Lord in his suffering brothers and sisters.

'Whilst I spoke,' continued Mother, 'they were taking pictures
of me. But I did not care; I just went on talking, looking straight
in front of me, without moving my head.'

She was a good subject for the cameraman, who must have
shifted his camera from her wrinkled face to her sandalled feet,
the white saree with a blue border covering her head and
forehead right down to her eyebrows, her right hand holding her
prayer beads, the cross in evidence on her left shoulder; then back
to the expressive mouth, the straight looking eyes of a woman
with a single purpose and an iron will. She spoke simply,
without show; a deep conviction rang in her voice as she appeal-
ed to the viewers to understand and love those around them who
feel lonely or unwanted or who lack proper care. She made no
mention of money, issued no call for help in favour of her institutions. She stressed that even in well-to-do countries, boasting
an elaborate social welfare service, there were legions of persons
who looked in vain for love in their own homes, who craved
recognition or attention. Further, true love should also embrace

those people who belonged to other countries, races and cultures.

Many viewers of the T.V. interview were impressed. Donations for Mother's works poured in.

Malcolm Muggeridge was perhaps the person most impressed. Promoter and organizer of the drama, he had taken an active part in it. He brought a camera crew to Calcutta to make a film depicting the daily life and work of Mother and her Sisters. He stayed three days at the Mother-house, enjoying the freedom of the place. The crew filmed the Mass and the Sisters at prayer; the dormitories; the classrooms; the Sisters taking their meal; the clothes drying; the Sisters filling water buckets and carrying them up the stairs.

He visited the dispensaries, the Kalighat Home for the dying, the Children's Home, the leprosy clinics.

He made Mother talk – she spoke of God's action and goodness, and of the Sisters who worked as his instruments.

Muggeridge interviewed the Sisters. The faith of the nuns struck him and their devotion deeply moved him.

But for the Sisters it is a hard life of faith, the uneventful repetition of the same humble task day after day. Mother sees the beauty of their life, not with human eyes, but with the vision of faith God gives her. She has nearly reached perfect Christian joy and serenity, since, as she says 'We do it for Jesus,' it is all beautiful. And when she tells us in the Home for the dying 'God is here': her intuition sees him present as simply and obviously as she does the destitute.

But the Sisters, the Sick and Suffering, the Co-Workers and all of us, her friends, we have still to discover God's presence the hard way and work in pure faith as we carry the Cross after Christ. Mother knows it well when she speaks to her Sisters. Her great duty is to train them to constant self-denial, humility, service of the poor, love of God. Close to the great crucifix alongside the staircase of the Mother-house, I read the words: 'The miracle is not that we do this work, but that we are happy to do it.' This conviction Mother drills into the minds of the young novices. 'Be happy to do this work for God,' this disposition, which is neither natural nor easy, requires God's grace and help.

Mother Teresa was the first living Catholic nun privileged to appear on the cover of *Time*, in 1975. The caption was 'Living Saints' and the sub-title called them 'Messengers of Love and Hope'. The cover bore her portrait. The artist made the portrait on the basis of photos taken at the Mother-house. Mother Teresa confessed that during this ordeal she asked the Lord to deliver a soul from purgatory for every picture taken. On the cover she certainly looked like a sufferer and not at all as we are accustomed to see her, smiling, kind, serene in the certitude that the world moves constantly, if slowly, towards God. She seemed to bear the suffering of the world. It is one aspect of her personality: she knows suffering; but her faith makes her see the love of God calling men to himself. She brings joy wherever she goes and wants her Missionaries of Charity to do the same. The leading article depicted her correctly, as it stressed that her charity was fostered and sustained by an intense spiritual life.

The various awards and distinctions Mother Teresa has received also helped to make her work and that of her sisters more universally known, appreciated and supported.

In September 1962 Mother received the Padmashree Award from the President of India. Although this is not the highest Indian honour it was a remarkable sign of appreciation shown for the Mother's work.

This was the first time Mother was singled out in this way and the honour caused some difficulties. Archbishop Dyer asked whether he should let Mother Teresa go to Delhi to receive her Padmashree, as some priests feared she might feel some vanity at being thus noticed.

But others, who knew Mother well answered: 'Your Grace, have no fear, Mother does not know what vanity is. Just tell her that by honouring her the President means to honour all the religious who devote themselves to the service of the poor.'

On her side Mother was reluctant to be thus honoured and she asked the Archbishop 'I suppose I should not go to Delhi?' He answered her 'You must go, Mother.'

The Indian honour was followed by an international recognition: the Magsaysay Award given Mother by the President of the Philippines, who invited her to dine with him and his wife. This Award helped her to establish a Home at Agra and contributed to the knowledge of her as a well known inter-national symbol of Christian charity.

In 1971, there was a flood of prizes:
The Pope John XXIII Peace Prize given to Mother by Pope Paul VI; the Good Samaritan Award in Boston; the John F. Kennedy International Award; a Doctorate of Humane Letters in Washington.

In 1973 Mother went to the U.K. to receive the Templeton Award; the substantial sum of money it carries was immediately spent by her on a foundation for lepers. The Award was given her at a ceremony presided over by Prince Philip. At lunch she was seated next to Prince Philip: a slight nun in a coarse cotton saree next to the tall and smart Prince Consort. Both had at least one thing in common: like Mother, the Prince knows his own mind and speaks it publicly.

'Prince Philip was charming,' said Mother some days later. 'He had kind words to say about our Institute. During the meal he enquired about our work and I told him what we do and why we do it. They served only one course; I suppose it was out of consideration for me, and my work among the poor.' This was a thoughtful and tactful gesture in the best British tradition.

Here stood, in this modern world of comfort and luxury, a liv-ing replica of John the Baptist. Her cheap dress, her sandalled feet, her hands fingering the rosary, her direct speech, her single-mindedness reminded all of the Kingdom of God she was announcing. She stood as an index finger raised up high, pointing to heaven. Her smallness and humility raised her above the powerful of the world, whom she lifted up spiritually. Her very example made them cut down their pleasures and comfort, that they might share their wealth with the poor. In the breast of many arose a clearer consciousness of the needs of their brethren, as Mother reminded them of the words of Christ which were the cause of her service to the poor: 'What you have done to the least of my brethren, you did it unto me.'

13. Mother Teresa Speaks

On the fifteenth of October, eight days after the Missionaries of Charity had celebrated their Silver Jubilee, I had an hour long talk with Mother, a very personal, spiritual, intimate talk. She was perfectly relaxed, serene. It is extraordinary how quickly she had recovered after the heavy exertions of the Jubilee, when she looked pathetically tired and physically exhausted. Now she was fresh and smiling as she spoke.

She was to deliver a speech at the U.N.O. Temple of Religions on the 24th October. She wanted to describe the essential characters of the Christian religion. Her speech was to begin: 'God is Love'. Love in himself, a wonderful process of life, of giving and receiving, of sharing the divine Essence. God creates us out of love; the Father sends His Son to save the world out of love, 'God so loved the world that He gave His only Son that the world might live' (*John 3, 16*).

The Son gives his life and dies for us out of love for mankind. The Spirit Jesus sends us is the Spirit of Love, the Bond of Love between the Father and the Son; He comes to unite us to Jesus and to one another in love. Then, Christ commands us to love one another; and our service to our brethren, who are first the brothers and sisters of Jesus, is a service of love. We serve Christ especially in the needy and the poor, but also in all men, out of love for Him. That love will be all the more perfect if we allow the Lord to live in us and love in us with the perfection of His love.

Mother could close her eyes or look straight before her at nothing or nobody in particular, let the Lord speak and explain this Catholic vision of brotherly love, and the great need men have of it today. That was what the public expected from her. But we agreed that the theological foundation of her vision of love had to be clearly expressed.

Mother took notes, adding to her outline. Then she closed her file.

'When are you leaving?' I asked her.

'Tomorrow I leave for Rome, where a Jubilee Mass is to be celebrated by a Cardinal.'

'Will you go to see the Holy Father?'

'If he calls for me; otherwise I shall not go. After that I fly to New York. I shall stay with the Sisters in our house in Harlem.

'There are times,' she said suddenly, 'when I feel absolutely empty; an empty shell; a thing without consistence, with nothing in me to support me; I feel so lonely and miserable.'

'Yes, and still you go on working for God's glory. It is as St Paul said: "By myself I can do nothing; but I can do all things through him who strengthens me." '

I said this to console her. But I thought of St John of the Cross, and understood what she meant. At times God tries us; at times He gives us a share in the dereliction of Christ at Gethsemane. God seems absent; He withdraws from the soul all consolations and all feeling of His Presence. We must plod on in sheer faith; a faith no more felt, dumb, cold and lifeless.

'Yes, Mother, whoever loves God must pass through the dark tunnel — sometimes more than once; perhaps often and for a long time.'

The fact is well known; the details, the frequency and intensity of the trial vary according to God's plan.

We remained silent for a while, before the mystery of God's work in souls.

Then I asked her:

'When I speak to the Tertians, Mother, on what point do you want me to insist especially?'

'Insist on prayer,' she said. 'In prayer they must find God, find strength to live their vocation and be faithful to it.'

'Yes, in all your chapels on the wall is inscribed the call of our Lord "I Thirst".'

In Yemen 'I THIRST' in English and Arabic.

In Gaza 'I THIRST' in English and Hebrew.

In Rome 'I THIRST' in English and Italian.

'In every house of ours, you enter the chapel and you see "I THIRST!" The call of Jesus. We exist to console Jesus, to quench His thirst for love. It is our function, our aim.

'I pray to our Lord that if the Sisters are not to be faithful to their vocation, he may let the Institute die. God can do without us. The Church would go on existing without us. If the Sisters are not faithful to their religious calling, our Lord may suppress our Congregation.'

'They will be faithful, Mother, I assure you. Our Lord will keep them close to His heart; He will not let them go astray. Your prayers and your blessings will help them.'

'Yes, the Sacred Heart. In Latin America, we consecrate families to the Sacred Heart of Jesus. The Sisters prepare groups of forty or fifty families, regularise marriages, prepare the children for their first Communion. Then, when all are ready, they solemnly enthrone a picture of the Sacred Heart in the house. Is that not wonderful! Our Lord comes to reign over those families, to sanctify them. He brings love in their midst. But first, they must be religiously married, otherwise there is no enthronement. The family must be established on a firm basis to receive God's blessing.'

'Latin America, what a field for your apostolate – such poverty, misery, ignorance, but also such good will, and desire for spiritual values. Mother, do all in your power to spread there. I wish the bishops would call you more earnestly. Your Sisters have the right approach to many of those who live in material and spiritual need in Latin America. Will you open a house in Mexico, now?'

'No, later. Things are not ready as yet.'

'I shall come back via Africa. We have already nineteen African novices and postulants. Excellent vocations. They are keen to devote their lives to our Lord.'

'You should open a novitiate there and train your African Sisters in their own environment, culture and tradition. Later you can bring some of them here that they may have the genuine spirit of your Society.'

'We have already two African novices in India. Three are in Rome, and the postulants remain in Africa. Travelling is expensive; it costs much to bring them by air from another continent.'

'Have you any financial problems?'

'Money? I never give it a thought. It always comes. We do all our work for our Lord; He must look after us. If He wants something to be done, He must give us the means. If He does not provide us with the means, then it shows that He does not want that particular work. I forget about it.'

To the same question put to her some fifteen years earlier, she had given exactly the same answer. So that was truly a part of her attitude in life, her trust in God, her assurance that he looked after this small Society. She took our Lord at His word in this matter of material means. Thus a great source of worry and anxiety was removed from her mind, allowing her perfect freedom of thought and action. Having put her full trust in God, she abandoned herself to His holy guidance in all she did, thought, said and taught.

'Mother, do you still personally know all the Sisters and novices?'

'Not the novices. But I know all the professed Sisters.

'I write to them all. Last year one hundred and fifty three took their vows. I wrote a personal letter to each one of them, giving them advice on spiritual matters. They also write to me.'

'So, that is what you do in the evenings! You must write a huge number of letters.'

She smiled.

I thought of the one hundred and fifty-three fish caught in the apostles' nets after the Resurrection of our Lord, as recorded by St John: 'Simon Peter went abroad and dragged the net to the shore, full of big fish, one hundred and fifty-three of them; and in spite of there being so many the net was not broken.' (John 21, 11) This was of course an image of Peter's future work, which was to bring men into the Kingdom of God, as followers of Christ. Mother would also catch both women and men and bring them into the Kingdom of God.

January 1976: Mother was back from America, Europe, Africa.

'Each time I go to Europe and America,' she said, 'I am struck by the unhappiness of so many people living in those rich countries: so many broken homes, children not looked after by their parents. Their first duty is to work among their own people, bring together separated couples, build good homes where the children may receive their parents' love.

'They have material wealth; they lack spiritual values.

'Then there are the mentally handicapped. Have you met Jean

Vanier? You must meet him. A fine man. He established *l'Arche*, a home for mentally retarded persons. We must work with him, start a home for these people in Calcutta.'

'His organization is completely different from yours, he works with volunteers, free to come and go when they wish.'

'I met some of them and this is what I understood. But their aim and spirit resemble ours: both manifestations of Christian charity.'

'Did you meet them in Canada?'

'Yes, earlier they invited me to Toronto and I spoke to them there. I came back via Africa to visit our house in Ethiopia and the two houses in Tanzania. Africa is a land of promise. There is much poverty there, but also a large field of apostolate. We have excellent prospects. We are going to open a novitiate in Africa, at Tabora. Some twenty African girls want to join us. Four are on their way, to join the novitiate here. After a year I shall send them back with four Indian Sisters and start a house of formation there. They are very keen to work with us.

'In London seven postulants have joined. One Belgian girl has joined; she is the first from that country. Others are from the U.K., France, the U.S. In Melbourne, we have three Chinese novices, and already some candidates from Papua. In Yemen, thirty Moslem girls have refused to marry, and want to work with our Sisters. As Moslems of course, otherwise it would not be tolerated.'

'Where are you opening new houses?'

'I am going to the Philippines to open a house in Manila. The Archbishop is very keen on our settling there.'

'You will have plenty of spiritual work in the Philippines. The people are in the majority Catholic, but the number of priests is very small. There are more than 5000 Catholics to each priest.'

'Why is that?' she asked.

'Well, there is a scarcity of vocations, as in South America. People are baptized but many do not attend Mass or receive the sacraments. Perhaps your Sisters will be able to improve matters, at least in a small manner.'

'We have also been invited to South Korea.'

'Go to Korea, Mother. Go by all means. The Church is growing fast in that country and has a tremendous future. But we must not delay.'

She did not know this. I wondered how then she could decide where to open new houses to the best advantage. Was she sure of the guidance of the Holy Spirit in every case? She did ask advice from some priests. She had her counsellors, but mistakes had been made in the choice of locations.

'Why do you do so much for Darjeeling diocese, a relatively small diocese, as far as population and the number of Catholics are concerned, with a high ratio of priests and nuns to the population?'

'We are going to open a new house in the diocese, at Gangtok, the capital of Sikkim. The Bishop is very keen on our going there. The Church is not represented in this small town.'

'I know many people are well disposed towards the Catholic Church and some are asking for instruction. I said Mass in the palace of the Chogyal of Sikkim some years ago. But we have no church there as yet. Tell me, have you a soft corner in your heart for Darjeeling? Is it because you made your novitiate there or because you got your inspiration in the train on the way to that hill station?'

'No,' she said, brushing away the idea with a gesture of her hand.

'Then has the Bishop mesmerised you?'

She laughed. 'Go to see Takdah,' she said, 'a new house has been given to us there.'

That was a cogent argument. When a property suitable for her work is presented to her, then Mother is inclined to accept the gift. She sees the hand of God in the offering of the property for the Sisters' work.

'Mother, what do you consider most important in the training of your Sisters?'

'Silence. Interior and exterior silence. Silence is essential in a religious house. The silence of humility, of charity, the silence of the eyes, of the ears, of the tongue. There is no life of prayer without silence.'

'Yes, Mother, we need silence to find God, and hear him speak to the soul.'

'Silence,' she said, 'and then kindness, charity; silence leads to charity, charity to humility. Charity among themselves, accepting one another when they are different; charity for union in a community. Charity leads to humility. We must be humble.

'It strikes me how God is humble. He humbled Himself; He who possessed the fullness of the Godhead took the form of a servant. Even today God shows His humility by making use of instruments as deficient as we are, weak, imperfect, inadequate instruments.

'Then, there must be joy in the heart, the joy of serving God, the joy of doing His work. That is not incompatible with humility.'

'Indeed, in her Magnificat, Mary exclaimed that she rejoiced "because He who is mighty has done great things to me!" '

'Yes, I tell the Sisters not to fear to do good before the eyes of men. Our Lord said "Let your light shine before men, that seeing your good deeds they may praise your Father in heaven!" So, let men see your good deeds: it is Christ who does them through you.'

'Father, when they praise us for what we are doing, I do not mind it at all; rather, I rejoice because it all leads to the glory of God.'

'You have just returned from Kerala, Mother. Did you visit all your houses?'

Mother did not answer for a moment. She frowned slightly. I thought I sensed some diffidence or disappointment in her voice, as she answered:

'We have five houses there. People used to look down upon the Sisters because we work for the poor. Now we start to be accepted.'

'You are getting plenty of vocations from that State.'

'Yes. But I want to keep a good mixture. Many novices come from Bihar and Orissa. Vocations also come from Tamil Nadu. We were invited to go to a place where there are eleven hundred temples. A real citadel of Hinduism, very orthodox, with no Christian influence. The Archbishop was very happy when he heard it and he requested me to accept.

'I have to go to Santiniketan to receive a degree. I don't know why universities and colleges are conferring titles upon me. I never know whether I should accept or not; it means nothing to me. But it gives me a chance to speak of Christ to people who otherwise may not hear of him.'

In fact, universities or institutions, especially perhaps the less known ones, sometimes make use of the world-famous Mother Teresa to get into the news. At the start Mother may have been helped by this publicity; but not any more.

'I have also been asked to speak at the Philadelphia Eucharistic Congress in July.'

'That is a reward for your deep devotion to the Blessed Eucharist. You already spoke at the Eucharistic Congress in Melbourne.'

'Yes, but this time it will be more complicated. This is an eight day affair, and they want me to speak every day on all kinds of subjects.'

'Well, the Lord will come to your help as usual.'

'Here is Sister Dorothy, who is leaving for Australia to take over the office of regional Superior.'

I felt very unworthy to give a blessing to these two women whose prayers I needed more than they needed mine, but they trusted in the priestly power conferred by Christ. Still, I suggested that we first pray together. We fell on our knees and I prayed aloud; 'Lord bless the Missionaries of Charity at work in Australia, make them holy, send them chosen candidates, bless those to whom they minister, and bless us all.' Then I blessed Sister Dorothy, and Mother Teresa kneeling by her side.

February 1976: 'I have just come from a meeting of the Calcutta Co-Workers, said Mother. I told them: "Holiness is not a luxury – you are all invited to it." I said this to Hindus, Moslems, Jains, Parsees, Christians.

'They seemed pleased to hear it. I developed the theme in this way. Holiness is to love God and love men. It is therefore not a luxury reserved for a few favoured persons. All are invited to be holy. I told them also that the Sisters need their prayers to be able to do their work; that the poor need their help, their understanding, their love. We all have much to give, to share, to contribute wherever we find ourselves to be living. Holiness starts in the home, by loving God and those around us for His sake.'

'Yes, Mother, you spoke rightly; holiness is not a luxury

reserved for a few chosen ones. Still, in practice, real holiness is
fairly rare.'

I groped for the text of St Peter which so well applies to the
Sisters Mother must train and to all the Co-Workers she inspires
and encourages on the way to holiness: 'Be holy in all you do,
since it is the Holy One who has called you, and Scripture says:
"Be holy because I am holy." These are the words of God, since
he is holy, he wishes those who belong to him to be like him.' (*I
Pet. 1, 15*)

Mother still felt the pain caused by one of the Sisters who had
left the Institute.

'Happily the cross is still there in your life, otherwise Jesus
might not recognize you,' I said.

'Yes, we follow Christ, we hear his words "I thirst." So many
people still misunderstand us; they take us for what we are not,
for social workers.'

'You are certainly not at fault when this happens; you tell
them clearly enough that you are first religious women consecrated to the service of God.'

February 1976: Bishop James Toppo of Jalpaiguri was in the
parlour with us.

'We are preparing new foundations,' said Mother.

'We are opening a house at Jalpaiguri, where his Lordship has
a property ready for us.

'I am just back from Gangtok, the capital of Sikkim. We intend to open a house there shortly.

'And yesterday three Sisters left for Mexico.'

'As a result of your meeting with the President last year?'

'Yes. They have a house ready for us. Later on I shall send a
few more Sisters. Some Sisters are also going to . . . what is the
name of that country which was recently badly shaken by an
earthquake?'

'Guatemala,' I volunteered. 'The people are practically all
Catholics, but there are few priests in the country.'

I was happy to hear that the Sisters were broadening their bases
in Latin America. And their experience and efficiency in

organizing relief in areas afflicted by natural calamities would serve them well.

'Then,' Mother went on, 'we are starting in Manila. Already several girls from the Philippines have asked to join us.'

'Wonderful. You really have the Lord's blessing. I hope you will soon have a network of houses there. The Philippines suffer from a great scarcity of priests.'

'Why is that?'

'It is due to political and other reasons. The people have a solid Catholic tradition and a deep devotion to Our Lord and to his Blessed Mother. You can build on that foundation. You should get many good vocations from that country.'

March 1976: As I enter the parlour, Mother is talking to an elderly gentleman.

'Father, meet Dr Gupta.'

As we exchange greetings, Dr Gupta tells me that his son was my student in the Economics Honours class. So we are no strangers.

'Carry on, Mother. I do not want to interrupt your conversation with Dr Gupta.'

'Sit down, Father.'

'Mother,' says Dr Gupta, 'I own a property which I would like to donate to you for your work. I cannot put up a large building, but I shall get some friends to contribute to the expenses. The property is situated on a road near DumDum.'

'Wonderful, Dr Gupta. We have a house at DumDum. The Sisters could go and work in your property. We might establish there an Asha Niketan — a House of Hope — for mentally retarded people.'

I give Dr Gupta my address and invite him to call; then I take leave, as it is time for my talk to the Tertians.

Two days later Dr Gupta comes to see me.

'How did you come into contact with Mother, Doctor?'

'Well, it happened like this. A young woman belonging to a respectable family was brought to me for delivery. Since she was not married, the family would not accept the child. Her parents asked me to find a suitable place for the baby. I had heard of Mother; so I called at her convent. She was absent, but the Sister-

-in-charge was very kind. She immediately said that this was their work; they would take the child any day I chose to bring him. They would look after the baby and eventually get him adopted. This act of kindness struck me much. Since then I try to help the Sisters in whatever way I can.'

This was wonderful. Good people were coming spontaneously to offer their help, to share their property with the poor.

March 1976: 'More and more often,' says Mother, 'I am requested to speak in public. This is an ordeal for me; I wish I did not have to do it.'

'How do you manage to speak, Mother.'

'I close my eyes and I do this,' she answered, making with her right thumb a small cross on her lips. 'Then I let him speak. I follow his inspiration.'

'Do you look at your audience?'

'No. I look straight in front of me, above their heads. I look at no one. I deliver my message.'

She remembers what Christ promised 'When you stand before kings and judges, do not worry about what you are to say.'

Still, when she has been warned that she will have to address a gathering, it would be tempting God to go completely un-prepared – that would not be trust but presumption. Her listeners today are not judges and enemies, but friends and sympathizers, who appreciate this opportunity to hear the Word of God. Mother always speaks of God and Christ.

She goes forth in the power of the Lord, as the young David faced Goliath, without embarrassing himself in armour not made for him; he took his sling and five pebbles. God guided his arm and gave him strength. Mother does the same; her words, like pebbles, strike men's minds and shake them out of their ig-norance and complacency. They do not kill; they vivify, awaken, stimulate good impulses and generous actions. She can say, like Paul to the Corinthians, that she does not appeal to human wisdom, but only to knowledge of Christ Jesus. 'As for me, when I came to you, brothers, it was not with any show of oratory or philosophy, but simply to tell you the testimony of God. The only knowledge I claimed to have was about Jesus, and only about him as the crucified Christ.'

As Paul confesses: 'Far from relying on any power of my own, I came to you in great fear and trembling'; (*I Cor. 2, 1–5*) so does Mother, who finds public speaking a most painful and trying exercise; yet for God's honour, she accepts to do it. Like Paul she strikes the minds of her audience because she is filled with Christ.

She talks in a homely, simple, but forceful way. Her speech elevates, yet remains always practical and adapted to the audience.

After my instruction to the Tertians, Mother said:

'We shall take you home, Father. The van is going to the station with the Sisters who take the night train for Kalimpong. We are opening a house there.'

The Sisters sang a hymn in honour of those leaving for Kalimpong. Then the latter went into the van waiting outside, full of luggage; somehow they all managed to squeeze in. I sat next to the driver; Mother sat just behind me.

'We always sing when Sisters leave,' she said.

As the van started Mother led the prayers for a safe journey, and we all answered. The last invocation was as usual 'Immaculate Heart of Mary, cause of our joy, pray for us.' Mary brings joy to the world in the person of Jesus, her child. And now serving Christ in the poorest of the poor, the Sisters put the accent on 'joy'.

We made for the station. On the way Mother spoke of the new foundations she was preparing.

'God,' she said, 'is good to the Institute. The Sisters are invited in many places; we cannot accept all the requests. More Sisters are needed. We must pray for vocations.'

When we reached Scaldah station, the Sisters unloaded the mattresses, blankets, buckets, bags of foodstuffs and all that they were taking with them for the poor.

'We carry all our goods ourselves,' said Mother, laughing. 'They call us the coolie-sisters, because we always do without porters.

'I shall go up to Kalimpong in a few days, when the Sisters have settled down and I can see better what their needs are. They will have discovered what kind of work is more urgent.'

Thus Mother goes from one foundation to another, spreading her work of love always farther into new cities and new countries.

But even in its vast extension this work remains centered on the human person, as Mother shows her concern for the spiritual and material welfare of the individual.

Every human being counts for her; she sees not crowds but faces revealing human souls to her.

14. The Jubilee

'First I thank my God through Jesus Christ for all of you and for the way
in which your faith is spoken of all over the world.'

(Rom. 1, 8)

On a Sunday in October 1976 at the Cathedral of the Most Holy
Rosary, the Archbishop concelebrated Mass with a large number
of priests in thanksgiving to God for the blessings He had
bestowed on Mother Teresa and her Missionaries of Charity and
through them on such large numbers of Christians and non-
Christians.

Members of many religious institutes united their prayers to
those of the Sisters; children and adults, instructed by the Sisters,
benefactors, helpers, all thanked God for the Congregation and
the good it had effected.

On Monday, Mother Teresa and one of her Sisters came to the
Sacred Heart Church, to invite Monsignor Barber and myself to
concelebrate the Mass of the next day, a Mass to mark the Silver
Jubilee of the Missionaries of Charity, a great day of joy and
thanksgiving. As she sat upright in her chair, as usual, I noticed
how tired she looked. Yet she talked cheerfully with us for an
hour and a half.

'I am so grateful to you and to your father,' Mother told Monsignor Barber. 'Your father was the first to help me when I left
Loreto and started this work.'

'You must be very tired, Mother?'

'Yes, but it was all wonderful. People prayed for us and with
us; thanked God for what he had done through the Missionaries
of Charity. These last days, we went every day to pray in some
temple or church. The Archbishop gave us permission to do so.
We prayed with the Jews, the Armenians, the Anglicans, the
Jains, the Sikhs, the Buddhists, the Hindus. It was extraordinary.

All hearts united in prayer to the one true God, thanking Him for the great things He has done through his servants.'

'Yes, this is the spirit of the Magnificat in which Mary exclaimed 'My soul praises the Lord and my spirit rejoices in God my Saviour: because He has done great things to me and holy is his name.'

'Yes. We did nothing; He did everything. All glory must be returned to Him.

'Today we were with the Jains in one of their temples. There were four Jain priests who wore no clothes. They sat behind a table.'

'You have been so long in India and you do not know the habits of the Jain priests of the Digambara sect?'

'No. Whilst they were reading from their Scriptures and praying to God, a woman clad in white, a nun, I think, was pulling out some of her hair. In a spirit of penance, I suppose. I tried also to pull out some hairs from my head. It is painful, you know.'

We all laughed. Mother's head is usually so well covered by the border of her saree, that I have never seen her hair.

After some more reminiscences, she spoke of the work. Truly she was indefatigable.

In October, on the feast of the Most Holy Rosary, on which the Congregation of the Missionaries of Charity had been approved by Rome twenty-five years earlier, a simple, intimate ceremony took place at the Mother-house. All over the world, in some eighty houses of the Congregation, in every continent, in Rome, Harlem, Tabora, Melbourne, London, Lima, Mauritius, Yemen, Jordan, Calcutta, Bombay, Madras, Delhi, Ranchi, among other places too numerous to name, prayers ascended to God in thanksgiving. The Sick and Suffering, the nuns in cloistered monasteries, the Co-Workers of many countries, joyfully sang their gratitude to God and asked him to bless abundantly the Missionaries of Charity during the next twenty-five years.

At six a.m., as I approached the Mother-house, I looked up; there were no clothes hanging to dry on the roof, as there usually were. On the street a milk distributor went on his rounds. People slept peacefully on the pavements. Before the house a discreet police service indicated that the Governor of West Bengal was coming to assist at the Mass at this early hour.

Some twenty priests prepared to concelebrate the thanksgiving Mass with the Archbishop of Calcutta. Father Van Exem was present; Father Henry did not come – he was praying in the church of St Teresa, not far away. Father Gorrée had arrived from France for the occasion.

The small chapel was filled to capacity. As the priests entered the chapel for Mass, they could see the crucifix hanging from the wall, and the inscription next to it, 'I THIRST'.

There were pews for the special guests. Mother and the Sisters knelt or sat on mats.

Archbishop Picachy expressed the gratitude of all present for twenty-five years of grace. He expressed the wish that the Sisters be holy and fully dedicated to the service of Christ their Lord.

As the Mass proceeded, words and songs of praise of God and gratitude were on all lips whilst peace, joy, serenity filled all hearts. The promise Jesus expressed in the Upper Room: 'I have told you this so that my joy may be in you and your joy be complete' (John: 15, 11) was realized. The Holy Spirit had come at Pentecost to fill the minds and hearts of all present, bringing his gifts: love for God and men, joy in the service of Jesus and his brethren.

The universality of the Society was manifest: Sisters coming from the six continents were present, eager to return to their posts for work.

In the afternoon, Mother went to Creek Lane, where she had received such heart-warming hospitality from Michael Gomes and his family, and climbed the stairs leading to the Upper Room. Mother brought the picture of Our Lady which had adorned the altar during the years of pure faith. She wished to thank their first helpers and hosts. She stayed ten minutes and left.

The next day, Mother was off to Cuttack, in Orissa, to start a new house there. It was again work as usual, and expansion throughout the world continued.

The Jubilee provided a fit occasion to sum up the results of twenty-five years of work under the direction of the Holy Spirit, of twenty-five years of extraordinary graces and blessings.

In India the Missionaries of Charity have been an unqualified success. The results have been beyond all expectations.

Mother Teresa is the best known and most loved, most widely respected disciple of Christ in the country. She personifies selfless love and service.

Before Mother and her Sisters appeared, the Catholic Church was mainly known as an educational organization; Mother has made the Church known as a charitable organization and as a force for social progress. It still requires a contemplative leader, inspired by the Spirit, to establish the Church before the public as a spiritual and mystical force, leading to the knowledge and experience of God.

During the years, Mother Teresa's fame in India has grown steadily. She has always professed to be first a religious, completely devoted to God's service, receiving her inspiration and strength from God. She has proved to be a model of Christian charity, selfless, caring for all, devoted, asking for and ready to accept the collaboration of others whatever their beliefs.

She has been noted for her quick decision, prompt action, and forceful implementation; and for her readiness to start difficult tasks even without the necessary means, in the certitude that God will provide them when the work is for his glory.

The Sisters, trained by her, imitate her simple, efficient, practical style; they constitute a highly mobile force always ready to render service in time of emergency or calamity.

Mother has worked in the Gandhian tradition – living simply, poor and frugal in her ways, keeping out of politics, working for the destitute, teaching self-help, making use of local resources. Joining prayer to work she proved always ready to assume the most unpleasant tasks.

In Latin America, a continent in many respects similar to India, a few outposts have been established. The Congregation started with great hopes, which have not yet materialized. Valuable spiritual help has been given; but this is still very little compared to the needs and possibilities of this vast area.

The Institute has half a dozen houses and plans to open a few more. But it has not yet taken roots there.

Latin America, with close on half the Catholic population of the world, suffers from a great scarcity of priests and nuns. Its peoples are hungry for religious teaching, leadership and manifestations. In most Latin American countries there is much poverty, a great inequality in the distribution of wealth, large families, numerous slums and terrible poverty in the cities. But there is also a deep Christian tradition on which to build. There are many people who are responsive to the right approach, devoted to *La Madre de Dios* and Jesus crucified.

In such circumstances the Missionaries of Charity could have been expected to succeed as well, or nearly as well as in India. Yet the response has been weak. Calls from bishops came slowly, and are not the numerous, earnest appeals we expected.

When reminded of this, Mother, always optimistic answered: 'We have two novices. Some girls are applying to join us.'

'Yes, Mother, but what is that among three hundred million people of Catholic tradition and belief, with enormous needs?

'You have struck no roots as yet. You have three houses in Venezuela, all right; one in Peru, one in Colombia, one or two elsewhere. But how does that compare with the multitudes, the needs, the possibilities?'

By the end of 1974 the Co-Workers were organized in only one country, Venezuela.

'Why did you fail to effect a real start there, as you did in India?'

The Holy Father himself asked Mother Teresa, in a private audience, to make a big effort to multiply her activities in Latin America. Why did the Sisters not succeed better?

A reason may be the present efforts of some young priests to unite Jesus and Marx; the stress put on economic well-being and social justice rather than on faith in Christ and in the sacramental life; the bent towards political action and revolution, sometimes through violent means; the capitalistic structures which are considered the root of the evil, rather than the sin, pride, greed and sensuality which create them; the move towards Communism.

The Missionaries of Charity are outside politics and care not at all for these preoccupations. When in the United States Mother Teresa was asked 'Do you and your Sisters go in for politics?' she answered 'We have no time for them.'

This attitude in many countries is an advantage: the Sisters are suspected by none; they are concerned only with spiritual and charitable work. The Sisters' outlook is pragmatic; they are say-

ing, in effect: 'We do the work appointed to us; others may, discuss and prepare blue-prints for the society of the future.'

But perhaps people expect from the Sisters a greater degree of
adaptation to their life, culture, language. Can the 'Indian Sisters'
in Indian sarees catch the imagination of simple folk elsewhere?
Should the effort to become adapted to local conditions and the
mentality of the people Mother made so successfully in India, not
be repeated in Latin America? Various countries have distinctive
cultural features that affect their religious life and style.

The adoption of English as their common language has given
the Missionaries of Charity a certain universality: it has helped
them to spread smoothly in all the countries where English is the
language of the people or at least of the educated class. But in
non-English speaking countries progress was modest. Should
English remain the Society's usual language in Spanish or
French-speaking countries?

'A bishop asked me,' said one of the Sisters who came back
from Venezuela, 'Why do you not adopt Spanish as your community language?'

In Africa, a good start has been effected. Prospects are bright,
possibilities of work enormous, whilst many vocations can be expected from the English-speaking countries of Africa.

The numerical increase of the Missionaries of Charity, though
very remarkable, should not be considered exceptional. On the
day of the Jubilee, the Sisters numbered 1133, including more
than 200 novices.

The progress of the Franciscan Missionaries of Mary, whose
Mother-house is at Ootacamund in South India and whose story
resembles that of the Missionaries of Charity, was still more spectacular. When they celebrated their silver jubilee, the institute,
founded in 1877 by Mother Mary of the Passion, numbered about
3000 members.

Both Congregations wish to offer signal service to God. The
Franciscan Missionaries of Mary add to the religious vows of
poverty, chastity and obedience a promise to offer themselves as
victims of love to Christ. The Missionaries of Charity take a

fourth vow to dedicate themselves to the service of the poorest of the poor.

St Paul wished to go to the ends of the world, at least to one end. He planned to visit Spain, considered as it was one extremity of the inhabited world by the ancient Greeks and Latins. He may not have succeeded in reaching Spain, though he saw many countries and preached the faith in more places than anyone in his time.

Mother Teresa was more fortunate; with the same desire, to spread the message of Christ, His work, His influence, as far as possible, she went to the extremities of the world. How otherwise would one explain her keenness and happiness to open a house in Papua, to go to places as widely apart as Fiji, Mauritius, New York?

Still, like Paul she would have to suffer some setbacks. Even after a spectacular development, half the world remained beyond her reach. She had not penetrated behind the Iron and Bamboo Curtains. The Chinese Communist world and the Soviet Communist world, close to one half of the earth's population, were out of bounds.

China, with her eight hundred million people, all God's children, looked like a dream country. Would she ever enter that Promised Land? Would the men in power really object to the Missionaries of Charity, unassuming, unsophisticated, unattached to any political system or ideology? The Sisters were certainly no spies, no revolutionaries, nor did they forward the interest of any foreign country.

Two Chinese Sisters had joined in Calcutta, three more elsewhere. Houses were opened in Taiwan, Macao, Hong Kong, perhaps as stepping stones; one day the Sisters might cross into the mainland of the Celestial Land.

To China, yes, some day, they will go. Francis Xavier died facing the mainland, on Sancian Island, from where his body was brought back to Goa. The Sisters might go one step further; reach the mainland and enter it.

Would the second quarter of a century not see the Missionaries of Charity expand towards the East? Mother had gone East from her native land. Her Sisters had gone mainly West, when they left India.

I asked Mother:
'Are you in Japan?'
'No; but we have a girl who applied to join us.'
'Are you in South Korea?'
'No, but we may go there.'

Now, with a footing in the Philippines, the Sisters can spread eastwards. The Philippines offer a solid Catholic basis and a promise of many vocations. From there they will be able to go to Taiwan, Hong Kong, Indonesia, Japan, South Korea, and even China, in God's own time.

The most admirable result of Mother and her Sisters' apostolic activity is the tremendous number of acts of love for God and the neighbour they have caused to be produced. Acts of love originating from poor and rich, young and old. Acts of love – many of them of heroic quality, coming from the dying destitute whose last words had been 'My God I love you,' or 'Thank you, Sister.'

The acts of love and devotion of children all over the world who went without a meal, an ice-cream or a picture to help some poor brother or sister in some unknown town or village.

The acts of love of viewers of a T.V. programme, of listeners at a meeting, of readers of newspapers and magazines, showed and told the beautiful example of a life-long commitment to the service of Jesus in the poor, and responding to it.

The acts of love of Co-Workers, Sufferers, Helpers, many of them performed in an humble and unobtrusive way.

Countless acts of love of God, forming an uninterrupted chain and encircling the world, as Mother had envisioned in an early letter, when her whole community could still fit within a single room. But could even she foresee the wonders God would work through his weak instruments?

The Future

'After Mother Teresa, what next?' Many asked the question after the glorious days of the Silver Jubilee.

Mother seems to be so indispensable; the whole edifice she has built up appears to rest on her shoulders. She is Atlas carrying the world. The public and the officials know of her above all. Nearly everyone speaks of 'the Sisters of Mother Teresa,' whilst acknowledging her unique charism. This God-given charism is granted to an individual, not to a group. She believed, remained faithful, divested herself of all human self-love to belong to God, entirely; in her Christ lives and acts in a special manner.

What will happen after her? Charisms are not inherited; God dwells in the individual soul; mystical graces are personal. Then, in the world we know, hero-worship is directed to a person, though influence may belong to a group. After Mother Teresa, what will happen to her Institute?

'If the Society is God's work, it will endure,' said Mother. 'But if the Sisters are not to be faithful, if they are not to work for God's glory, then God may as well suppress the Society,' she added with determination.

Mother does not wish to see her own particular work extended and continued, but the name of the Lord proclaimed and glorified. This concern should obtain the graces necessary for her Society to continue after her.

Mother said: 'If the Society is God's work.' Is it presumptuous to affirm that the Society *is* God's work? The Institute has been officially approved by the Church; it has been blessed and commended repeatedly by the Holy Father, and by many cardinals and bishops; it is daily praised by the voice of the people, which is certainly in this case the Voice of God.

Men of all nationalities, social classes and religions are united in admiration for the works of charity performed by the Sisters.

'After Mother Teresa, what next?' ask many of her friends and collaborators. 'Will all this good work come to a standstill? Will the Sisters be able to carry on their apostolate without her leadership, guidance and support?'

To dispel all lingering doubts concerning this matter, I went to the Darjeeling Children's Home run by the Missionaries of Charity. It dominates the town, standing on a hill, two thousand metres above sea level. As I climbed up, I waved my hand to children playing on the roof. One of them ran down to open the door for me, then went to call a Sister.

'This building is new,' said the Sister who took us round. 'Two years ago we had here a shed that was destroyed by a violent storm. So we rebuilt this part of the building. The people helped us; the District Magistrate also.'

We went through the different rooms, which housed about a hundred inmates.

'All these children suffer from malnutrition. We feed them, give them vitamins and injections to make them strong. Many have wounds.

'This girl is sixteen years old; when she arrived she had a large sore on her leg. Now the wound is closed and healing. It was due to malnutrition. This girl has a stunted arm; this one is mentally retarded.

'We have ten orphan boys I sent as boarders to the Pedong High School; we must pay eighty rupees per month for each boy. We have also twenty orphan girls studying at the Bethany and St Teresa's Convent Schools close by; these come home for the night.

'Here is an old lady who is close to death.'

The lady, who was not a Christian, recognized me as a priest and asked for a blessing. I blessed her. The other ten or twelve inmates also asked for a blessing. We said a short prayer together and I blessed them.

'One person died the other day,' said Sister. 'Come this side; there are more children. Some are total orphans, others have one parent living. Either the father is at work and cannot look after the small children or the mother is too poor to feed them. One woman has four children here; a widow, working for a very small salary; she could not keep her four children. They all suffered from T.B. and malnutrition. Now they are picking up. This boy here seems to have no intelligence; he does not react to anything you say. We are trying to find out if he really is mentally deficient. With better food he may improve.

'Many of these cases come from the villages. We have a van and go down to the valley for dispensary work once a week. We brought here some of the more needy children.'

As we reach the chapel, Sister tells me:

'You know this place, you gave us some instructions two years ago.'

'Yes, I remember the chapel. Let us say a prayer for these good people and for the Sisters who look after them.'

The chapel is the source of strength and the oasis of consolation in the midst of all this misery, and among the poor of the Lord.

The visitor who stays one hour in the Home, smiles at the

children, says a kind word, pats a cheek, gives a blessing, finds
this pleasant. But for the Sisters it is the same hard task from morning till evening, and sometimes at night, caring for sick children
and the dying destitute, not for one or two years, but for
their whole life, with never a break.

The only spot of beauty and intimacy in the house is the
chapel. It is as beautiful as they can make it; for the Lord dwells
there. I see two vases holding lovely white lilies, lilies for Jesus
present in the tabernacle, present in these suffering brothers and
sisters. Against the wall stands a large crucifix; above it are
written the words of Christ 'I Thirst'. The Sisters are daily
reminded of the call of Jesus that brought them here.

As we leave the chapel, I put to Sister the question for which I
had come to see her:

'Sister, does Mother Teresa come here often?'

'No, she has not come to Darjeeling for a long time.'

'Does she write to you often?'

'No, she is too busy. She writes very seldom.'

'Do you receive any supplies from Calcutta?'

'We receive some supplies from Catholic Relief Services, as
other charitable institutions do. Once a year I go to Calcutta to
get a supply of medicines.'

'Do you ask the Bishop for any help?'

'No, we do not ask the Bishop for any financial help. He sends
a priest from Bishop's house to say Mass for us daily.'

'Of course, he must look after your spiritual welfare. And did
you contract any debt on account of this new building?'

'No, we have no debt. We manage things by ourselves.'

'I see that you do it very well.' I took her leave and came back
singing on the road. I had the answer to the question so many
people were asking: 'After Mother Teresa, what next?' The
answer was simple:

'After Mother Teresa, the Missionaries of Charity.' This house
of the Sisters and many others like it were being run quite
smoothly without Mother's intervention or help. The Foundress
had succeeded in her main task. The well trained Sisters could
stand on their own feet and take over.

There remained to answer the question: 'After Mother Teresa,
who? Who will take the reins and guide the Society in its

progress?' The answer lay in the Constitutions that specified how the Society was to be governed.

Mother and Father Van Exem had created the pattern of government in conformity with church rules for religious congregations.

In 1975 the General Congregation of the Institute had appointed Mother as Superior General for six years. All the ballot papers, except one, bore Mother Teresa's name as their choice to direct the Institute for the next six years.

Father Van Exem, the presiding officer, destroyed the only differing ballot paper, so that only he knows for whom Mother voted.

When Mother Teresa becomes unable or unwilling to carry on as Superior General, the Sisters elect a new Superior according to the rules laid down in their Constitutions. This Superior will not inherit the personal charisms of the Foundress; but she will receive from God the graces necessary to carry out her duties of Superior General of the Missionaries of Charity .

15. It was Thirty Years Ago ...

September 1976
'How was the Eucharistic Congress in Philadelphia, Mother?'

'Very fine.'

'Did you have to speak many times?'

'Yes, they wanted me to speak everywhere. I went about with eight policemen around me the whole time. The people would have crushed me. . . . I am so small. It was my worst penance to be thus guarded all the time.'

'Was there much pomp? or did you feel in a real religious atmosphere?'

'There was no show of pomp, no display. It was simpler than the Congress at Melbourne. The great procession with four hundred thousand participants was very religious. Cardinal Knox knelt on a priedieu behind the monstrance of the Blessed Eucharist, carried on a float. The American people are very pious. There were groups of other, what do you call them?'

'Denominations, they say nowadays.'

'Yes, denominations, present at some of the functions. We washed each other's feet, exchanged the kiss of peace, broke bread and ate it together, but then when it came to the Eucharistic sacrifice, they fell back. This was very painful. At Mass they would not join us. When there was Communion to the Body and Blood of Christ they were not with us. That was painful.'

'Yes, the Eucharist is the sign and touchstone of unity. We are truly one around the altar where the Lord becomes sacramentally present. We must pray for unity, complete unity that we may truly form one body of Christ.'

'Your General made a beautiful speech at the Congress. I must quote it when I meet some of your Jesuits,' she chuckled, 'I must tell them to live more poorly and go to the poor.'

Soon she was back to her great preoccupation:

'We must work for souls; it is really souls that matter. I feel so happy when I can do good to souls.'

She had written this in her intimate letters to Jacqueline de Decker, thirty years earlier. Her hunger for souls had not abated; it had grown with the passing of the years.

'I think the Sisters also feel happy when they can do good to the souls. After all that is why we started looking after the dying, that we might help them think of God at their last moments and make an act of love of God before dying; we want them to die with God.

'I think the Sisters also see the souls behind the bodies and rejoice when they can do spiritual good.'

She said 'I think' with imperfect conviction.

'The work does not distract me from God,' she continued.

'I went to Mexico. We have opened a house there. When the Sisters go round, the poor do not ask them for clothes, do not ask them for food, they ask them:

' "Teach us the Word of God." '

'So the people ask to hear the Word of God. . . .'

'No, they don't ask to *hear*, they ask the Sisters to *teach* them the Word of God.

'The President himself made arrangements for our house there, not the government. Everything is well arranged.

'Mexico is a huge city. On the outskirts where they gather all the garbage brought by the conservancy department, some five hundred families live on the picking and sorting of refuse, as many people do here. I told the President to leave them to that work, that is what they can do. Make the surroundings better and improve the houses and let them go on with that work. Already the Sisters have started instructing the children for their first Communion.

'We shall buy five hundred New Testaments and distribute them to these families. The whole Bible is too expensive. Also it is too difficult for them. Is this not wonderful that the people are hungry for the Word of God? Of course, in Mexico Catholics have been persecuted; this may be the result. Even now priests and nuns are not allowed to wear clerical or religious dress. Our Sisters go about in their habit – nobody knows what the saree is. But they wear their cross.'

'But, Mother, it is such a pity. In many places God's children are hungry for spiritual food and no one is found to give it to them.'

'Things are better in Mexico than in South America.'

'You are not doing too well there?'

'We have only two vocations. Lima, Peru seems more promising than Venezuela. The poor hanker for spiritual things. Why must so many priests and nuns busy themselves with politics when their primary work is to teach the faith?

'Everywhere people tell us: speak to us of Jesus.'

'Did you not start a new congregation? The news came out in the papers.'

'Yes, the Sisters of the Word. They are a contemplative branch. They have three hours of prayer at home and one hour in the church. Then daily two hours to go out and speak of Jesus. Not public speaking in the squares or street corners, just to speak of Jesus to people who want to listen. People are eager to listen to those who speak of our Lord.

'I wish I could retire there among the Sisters and just live a contemplative life, just be with Jesus.'

'Not yet, Mother; you have still much work to do. Why did you start that branch in the U.S. and not here?'

'Because they are ready for it. Sister Nirmala is in charge. She will do very well. She has already seven candidates.'

'Is the aim to receive nuns who left their convent and wish to come back?'

'There may be some such cases, of people who wish to do penance and to join the Institute.'

'I suppose the Congregation will develop under the inspiration of the Holy Spirit.'

'Yes, And speaking of inspiration, today is 'Inspiration Day' the 10th of September. It was thirty years ago, in the train taking me to Darjeeling that I heard His call.'

'The call to serve Jesus in the poorest of the poor. And you obeyed his call. When did you come to this house?'

'I do not recollect.'

'Was it in February 1954?'

'Yes, about that time.'

'Did you go to pray to the Fatima Shrine to obtain the house?'

'Yes, I went at times with the Sisters, praying on the way.

'They had first told me about another house, which was to cost us eighty-five thousand rupees. As I did not have the money, I decided to offer the sum in Memorares to Our Lady. So we all started saying Memorares. Every Sister one thousand Memorares. I said the prayer thousands of times. But we did not get the house. Instead a person told me "there is a gentleman who has a suitable house; I shall take you to him." He did so, introduced me and then left. The proprietor was astonished. "I don't know that person, neither did I tell anyone that I wanted to sell the house. But I was contemplating doing so." The house came to one hundred and twenty-five thousand rupees. Monsignor Barber paid it out of the diocesan funds.'

'And you paid them back slowly.'

'Yes, I paid back two or three hundreds at a time.

'I did not pay Our Lady again in Memorares, I had paid her once.'

'And now, it has become too small. You should look for another house for another novitiate. The place is too crowded.'

'No,' she said.

'But then you will have to refuse candidates, since the numbers are always increasing and you really cannot accommodate more in this house.'

'Why not? The Sisters can sleep on the floor; the poor do it.'

'They require more space; you cannot train them properly in this manner.'

'I shall remove the postulants who are here and send them to Park Street. And the candidates can be first received in various houses to see our kind of work and life.'

'That will lighten the burden on this house. Even so, you may have to open another novitiate in India.

'No. They must all come to Calcutta.'

She thought that only in the historical Mother-house would they imbibe the real spirit of the Congregation.

'You should open a novitiate in the Philippines,' I suggested. 'Transfer there the one from Melbourne. And from the Philippines you can spread towards the Far East; Hong Kong, if you find a property, Taiwan, Indonesia, Korea, Japan.'

'There is plenty of scope there. And one day, China.'

'Yes, the Philippines would be better than Australia. We have only two girls from that country, and do not expect to recruit many.'

'In the Philippines you will have plenty of candidates. For the training of the sisters in poverty and in work for the very poor, Australia is not the place – the country is too rich.'

'You should see our work among the aboriginals; they are terribly backward; it is incredible the way they live.'

'But the style of life will be more similar in the Philippines to what the novices meet in the East and Far East, except perhaps in Japan, which has become a rich country. But of course you require the good will and support of the Bishops of the Philippines.'

'Yes, in the course of time we can open a novitiate in the Philippines, and of course one in Africa.'

'And how was Rome, Mother?'

'Wonderful. I saw the Holy Father, in private.'

'I had told you he would call for you.'

'There was nobody else. I talked to him as I talk now to you, just facing him and quite simply.'

'Did he enquire about your work?'

'He knows about it already. I spoke of the new Congregation, the Sisters of the Word. He sent a blessing to all the Missionaries of Charity, to all the Co-Workers, he gave a special blessing for the Sisters of the Word.'

'You had a meeting of the Co-Workers in Germany?'

'Yes, it was wonderful. There are eighty thousand Co-Workers now, twelve thousand in the U.S.'

'Did you meet Jacqueline de Decker? was she able to travel to Germany?'

'Yes, she runs the Sick and Suffering. Only the national Vice-Chairmen came to Germany. They had to pay their own passages. The organization did not pay for them I had told them to save the money during the year, that it be not a burden on their family budget. The Germans were marvellous; no one had to go to a hotel; they were all received in families. When we met they insisted on prayer; prayer meetings every week, or every second or third or fourth week.

'I told them to practise charity first in the home, then among neighbours, then in their locality, in their country and finally in the world. But first have a home where there is love and understanding. Love between the members of the family will bring happiness.'

The Angelus bell rang in the convent. We said the Angelus. Mother then said:

'In many places the poor are happy to hear the Angelus bell. In New York the poor complained to the Sisters: 'Why is it that we don't hear the Angelus now? We were happy to pray to Our Lady when we heard the bell rung, the announcement of the good news of the coming of the Saviour.' The Sisters asked the priest, who said he had no time to ring the bell three times a day, and the parish could not afford to pay a person to come and ring it. So the Sisters took up the duty 'We shall come and ring, Father' they said. And now the poor of that very difficult locality are happy that they can again pray the Angelus.

'The poor are hungry for God; they want to hear about Our Lord. They do not worry so much about material things; they want to hear that they have a Father in heaven who loves them.

'About the book, I must ask you, nothing personal, that is, no personality, no personal credit. He did it all. It is all His work.'

'Yes, you do not want any praise; all praise is reserved for God. But you may say with Our Lady in her Magnificat 'He has done great things to me and holy is his Name.' What the Virgin Mary said you may say also.'

She was right; she had no merit in the whole thing except that of having allowed God to work through her. Humility is truth, said St Teresa of Avila. All good comes from God. But looking back to the moment of her call on the Road to Damascus — rather, to Darjeeling — she could say with St Paul 'I have kept the faith God had reposed in me, I remained ever faithful to Him.' Then he did great things through His humble handmaid

'We are not channels,' I added, 'we are instruments. Channels give nothing of their own, they just let the water run through them. In our action we are instruments in God's hand.'

'Yes,' she said, 'I like the comparison. I feel like a pencil in God's hand.'

She looked for a stub of pencil on the table, but there was none. She made a gesture with her fingers: 'God writes through us, and however imperfect instruments we may be, he writes beautifully.

'In God,' she continued, 'I find two things admirable: His goodness and His humility. His love and His humility are striking. God is truly humble; He comes down and uses instruments as weak and imperfect as we are. He deigns to work through us. Is that not marvellous?'

'Yes, it all starts with the idea of the Incarnation. The Son of God assumes our human condition; He walks among us and works with us; He even accepts to die on a cross to atone for men's sins.'

I knew well that Mother did not want any praise. I had recorded as objectively as possible what I had seen and heard and felt during these years with her and her Sisters. I took my clue from St John writing to the second or third generation Christians: 'What we have seen and heard and touched of the Word of Life, that we make known to you, that you also may share in our fellowship;' yes, share our experience, and rejoice at the coming of the Lord, at his manifestation to men, at the wonderful works he performed and still performs for our spiritual good, to save us and sanctify us.

I had an obligation to my readers who wanted to know how this page of Church history had been written, how this spiritual saga, this wonderful story had started and developed under the guidance of the Holy Spirit. A senior Sister had suggested: 'Father, please write especially about the beginnings. Say how the Missionaries of Charity started, give us a book that may inspire the younger members, the future novices who have not known the first years. . . .'

'Yes, Sister, the years of pure faith, the heroic years. Those who will join you later on have the right to know how the Congregation started. There are two trunks full of documents still with Father Van Exem. They may perhaps be opened at the next Jubilee. They will reveal details of juridical proceedings, correspondence dealing with the establishment, the constitutions, the rules of the Missionaries of Charity. That is for the historians who will sift the material, when all those connected with the foundation are gone to their reward.'

I had written at Mother Teresa's request to tell those who wanted to hear the simple and beautiful truth about the origins and the purpose of the Missionaries of Charity. I tried to write soberly, critically, constructively. As the spiritual director and confessor of the Mother-house for many years, I had felt that the Spirit of God guided the young Congregation. I had spoken with Mother on spiritual matters; we had discussed various aspects of the work and new foundations.

And now, to crown it all, the Lord had been good to me. In ninety minutes, on the thirtieth anniversary of the Day of Inspiration when Jesus had called Mother Teresa to be more closely united to his divine Majesty, we had gone over the different phases of the Institute, and summed up one by one the chapters of this book. Mother had followed the lead and confirmed what was written. She had always remained single-minded in pursuing her aim; neither the substance nor the emphasis had changed over these thirty years. God had been good to her, he had been good to me.

The bell went for the community supper. I got up and took Mother's leave. She accompanied me to the door; we both folded our hands in parting in the Indian manner. Then she bent down low, very low, out of respect for the priestly character of the man who makes Christ present on the altar. Mother Teresa is a woman of faith.

'Be careful,' she said gently, as she opened the door leading to the narrow lane and remembered that I am half-blind, 'there are two steps.'